# Anchor Hocking

## DECORATED PITCHER AND GLASSES

### The Fire King Years

PHILIP L. HOPPER

Schiffer Publishing Ltd®

4880 Lower Valley Road, Atglen, PA 19310 USA

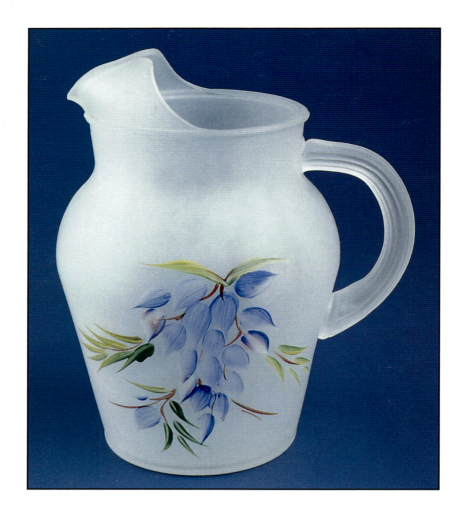

Designed by Bonnie M. Hensley
Cover design by Bruce M. Waters
Type set in Americana XBd BT/Zapf Humanist 601 BT

ISBN: 0-7643-1488-2 *2866 9074 10/02*
Printed in China
1 2 3 4

Published by Schiffer Publishing Ltd.
4880 Lower Valley Road
Atglen, PA 19310
Phone: (610) 593-1777; Fax: (610) 593-2002
E-mail: Schifferbk@aol.com
Please visit our web site catalog at
**www.schifferbooks.com**

This book may be purchased from the publisher.
Include $3.95 for shipping. Please try your bookstore first.
We are always looking for people to write books on new and related subjects. If you have an idea for a book please contact us at the above address.
You may write for a free catalog.

In Europe, Schiffer books are distributed by
Bushwood Books
6 Marksbury Avenue
Kew Gardens
Surrey TW9 4JF England
Phone: 44 (0) 20-8392-8585; Fax: 44 (0) 20-8392-9876
E-mail: Bushwd@aol.com
Free postage in the UK. Europe: air mail at cost.

# Dedication

I imagine that most people are bombarded and often overwhelmed by the events of the world each day as they try to get up, go to work, get through the day, hurry home to spend some time with the family, and still find some brief moments to relax and unwind. I think that some people have the natural ability to take everything in stride and weather any storm that might arise no matter how severe it is. As you travel through life, you meet these people and look with envy at their abilities. I think Dave Bates is such an individual.

I came to meet Dave through my decision to write books about Anchor Hocking glassware. In my quest to accurately document the company's glassware production, I turned to an expert for guidance. What better source of information could anyone ask for than someone whose job description included Anchor Hocking's glass composition control and melting services?

The foundation for Dave's glass expertise was laid on 2 February 1956 when he went to work for the Hazel Atlas Glass Company in Zanesville, Ohio. He worked in the physical testing laboratory testing glass from all ten Hazel Atlas plants. Shortly after the Continental Can Company purchased Hazel Atlas, the decision was made to move the laboratory to Plainfield, Illinois. Dave, however, had other ideas and preferred not to live in Illinois, so he joined the Anchor Hocking team on 19 December 1960. Over the next thirty-eight years, he would focus his work in two distinct areas: (1) physical testing and (2) composition control and melting services.

He spent the first seven years at Anchor Hocking in the physical testing area. The job responsibilities were similar to those he had at Hazel Atlas. The myriad of responsibilities included fracture diagnosis, viscosity measurements, hot and cold end testing, decoration testing (paint and decals), quality control test procedure training, and troubleshooting glass plant problems. In 1967, his job description was changed to composition control and melting services.

The new job would certainly test Dave's abilities as his responsibilities were expanded. This job covered seven distinct areas: (1) glass making raw materials, specifications and monitoring, (2) glass composition and batch calculations, (3) color control for both crystal and all colored glasses, (4) frit feeder operations including setup, color changes, and color control, (5) development of new colors to meet consumers demands and marketing changes, (6) working with plant personnel on color changes, tank drain, and fill or "on-the-fly" color changes, and (7) furnace setup, forehearth operation and solving production problems at other Anchor Hocking plants. Dave stayed in this new job until his retirement on 31 August 1998.

Now, with all this experience you can see why I went to him for help. I was lucky to find someone who also shared a love of glass, wanted to preserve Anchor Hocking's long and rich history, and was willing to share his knowledge with others. Not only did Dave provide me with most of the information concerning glass production methods at Anchor Hocking, but he was also kind and generous, donating several pieces of incredibly rare glass to the museum I built. I can't even begin to express all my gratitude to him for his expertise, sincerity, and generosity. Thanks for all your help!!!!

# Acknowledgments

I want to thank three very special people in my life. First and foremost is my wife Barbara. She has my "rock" and stood beside me during all the glass buying trips, packing and unpacking glass, photo sessions, and stress of writing several books. Next, I would also like to thank Susan Shaub for helping move glassware for four days during the marathon photo session for the decorated pitcher and glass books. Finally, I want to thank Bruce Waters for all his help in photographing the books, sorting the slides, and designing the book covers. Without these three people to help me, none of the books would have been possible. I thank them for their support and technical expertise.

We shot over 2,100 photographs in three days at my home in Texas. This feat required the transport of over 2,000 pieces of glass and 250-boxed sets from locations in the house to the photographic setup. After the photo session was over, all the glass was intact and nothing was broken! Unfortunately, as we were commending ourselves on this feat, I kicked a glass and it shattered into a million pieces. Still, one broken glass is a small price to pay for three books!

# Contents

# Foreword

I had a difficult time trying to decide how to organize this book to make it "user friendly." I finally decided to divide the book into three volumes: (1) one volume to cover the earlier years (approximately 1920 through 1950), (2) a second volume to cover the Fire King years (approximately 1950 to 1970) and (3) a final volume to cover everything made until the present day. I also tried to group the pitchers into decoration categories such as pitcher with stripes, juice pitchers, frosted pitchers, etc., since many of the decorations are not listed in catalogs and have no company decoration designation. In the later years, Anchor Hocking used three general styles of pitchers: (1) the 86 oz. upright pitcher, (2) the Finlandia style pitcher, and (3) the Chateau style pitcher. Some of the styles have been used for over 20 years and may still be in use. These three pitcher styles were originally made of colored glass without any decoration. In later years, the company added etching or enameled decorations. Then, the pitcher was given a name indicative of the added decoration and not the basic shape or style of the pitcher.

# Introduction

## Pricing

The prices in the book are only a guide. They are retail prices for mint condition glassware. Several factors will have an effect on glassware prices: regional availability, depth and consistency in coloring, the presence or absence of Anchor Hocking markings in the glass or as paper labels, and relative rarity of the piece. Certain items will command higher prices if they are sets in the original packaging. I would also consider labeled pieces (paper or marks embedded in the glass) to command a 10 to 20 percent increase in price over unmarked pieces. Prices will drop considerably for glassware that is chipped, scratched, cracked, or deformed. No matter what any reference book states, the bottom line is . . .

*Glassware is only worth what someone is willing to pay for it!*

## Measurements

I have tried to make this reference book as "user friendly" as possible. Too many times I have been in an antique shop and spotted a tumbler I wanted. The reference book I was using said this was a 12 oz. tumbler. Without a container of liquid and measuring cup I would have no way to actually determine if the tumbler held 12 ounces. I would rather know the tumbler is 5 inches high with a top diameter of 3 inches. This I can measure with a ruler. Unless otherwise noted, the measurements listed in the book are the height of the item. Realize, throughout the production of certain glassware items, the mold dimensions did vary. The measurements in the book are the actual measurements made on each piece of glassware pictured.

## Resources Available to Collectors

llectors today have a great variety of resources available. With the advent of the "electronic age," collecting capabilities have been greatly expanded. I can honestly state that this book would not have been possible without using the vast resources available, especially on the internet. Below I have listed the resources collectors can use for locating antiques and glassware; however, realize this list is not all-inclusive.

**Internet Resources:** Without leaving the comfort of your home or office, you can search worldwide for items to add to your collection. Presently, there are both antique dealers and auctions services on the internet.

eBay Auction Service: The eBay Auction Service provides a continually changing source of items. This internet service contains over 3,000,000 items in 371 categories. Internet users can register as both buyers and/or sellers. The majority of the items remain on the "auction block" for seven days. You can search the auction database for specific items. A list of items will be presented following the search. For example, you might want to find a Fire King Jadeite vase made by Anchor Hocking. Because the seller enters the item's description in the database, you often have to anticipate how the item is described. Don't limit the searches. In this case, you might have to search under Jadeite, hocking, fireking (no space), fire king (with the space), or vase to find the item you want.

Internet Antique Malls: There are several internet antique malls I have found to be extremely useful in locating glassware. Each mall contains numerous individual dealers with items for sale. The malls I used are listed below:

    1. TIAS Mall – (http://www.tias.com/)

    2. Collector Online Mall – (http://www.collectoronline.com)

    3. Facets Mall – (http://www.facets.net/facets/shopindx.htm)

    4. Depression Era Glass and China Megashow –

    5. Cyberattic Antiques and Collectibles – (http://cyberattic.com/)

**Glass shows, antique shops, and flea markets:** All collectors still enjoy searching the deep dark crevices of the local antique shops and flea markets. Many of the best "finds" in my personal collection were located in flea markets and "junk" shops. Most of the dealers in glass shows have a good working knowledge of glassware, so "real finds" are not too plentiful.

**Periodicals:** Both the *Depression Glass Magazine* and *The Daze, Inc.* are periodicals which will greatly enhance your collecting abilities. Along with the numerous advertisements for glassware, there are informative articles on all facets of collecting glassware.

**Word of Mouth:** This is one resource so often overlooked. Let others know what you are looking for. Consider expanding you search by including friends, relatives, and other collectors. This book could not have been written without the help of many fellow collectors.

Do not limit you collecting to only one resource. Remember the items you seek are out there . . . somewhere!

# Request for Additional Information

I am always seeking information concerning Anchor Hocking's glassware production. Much of the information about the company is not available in a printed format. This book will undoubtedly be updated and it is imperative new information be made available to collectors. If you have any information you would like to share with the "collector world," please contact me at the following address:

Philip L. Hopper
6126 Bear Branch
San Antonio, Texas 78222
E-mail: rrglass@satx.rr.com
Please be patient if you need a response. I am not in the glassware business. I am a military officer first and a collector the rest of the time. I will make every effort to provide prompt feedback on you inquiries. Include a self-addressed, stamped envelope if you desire a written response.

# History of Anchor Hocking

Anchor Hocking first came into existence when Isaac J. Collins and six friends raised $8,000 to buy the Lancaster Carbon Company when it went into receivership in 1905. The company's facility was known as the Black Cat from all the carbon dust. Mr. Collins, a native of Salisbury, Maryland, had been working in the decorating department of the Ohio Flint Glass Company when this opportunity arose. Unfortunately, the $8,000 that was raised was not sufficient to purchase and operate the new company, so Mr. Collins enlisted the help of Mr. E. B. Good. With a check for $17,000 provided by Mr. Good, one building, two day-tanks, and 50 employees, Mr. Collins was able to begin operations at the Hocking Glass Company.

The company, named for the Hocking River near which the plant was located, made and sold approximately $20,000 worth of glassware in the first year. Production was expanded with the purchase of another day-tank. This project was funded by selling $5,000 in stock to Thomas Fulton, who was to become the Secretary-Treasurer of Hocking Glass Company.

Just when everything seemed to be going well, tragedy struck the company in 1924 when the Black Cat was reduced to ashes by a tremendous fire. Mr. Collins and his associates were not discouraged. They managed to raise the funding to build what is known as Plant 1 on top of the ashes of the Black Cat. This facility was specifically designed for the production of glassware. Later in that same year, the company also purchased controlling interest in the Lancaster Glass Company (later called Plant 2) and the Standard Glass Manufacturing Company with plants in Bremen and Canal Winchester, Ohio.

The development of a revolutionary machine that pressed glass automatically would save the company when the Great Depression hit. The new machine raised production rates from 1 item per minute to over 30 items per minute. When the 1929 stock market crash hit, the company responded by developing a 15-mold machine that could produce 90 pieces of blown glass per minute. This allowed the company to sell tumblers "two for a nickel" and survive the depression when so many other companies vanished.

Hocking Glass Company entered the glass container business in 1931 with the purchase of 50% of the General Glass Company, which in turn acquired Turner Glass Company of Winchester, Indiana. In 1934, the company developed the first one-way, nonrefundable beer bottle.

Anchor Hocking Glass Corporation came into existence on December 31, 1937 when the Anchor Cap and Closure Corporation and its subsidiaries merged with the Hocking Glass Company. The Anchor Cap and Closure

Corporation had closure plants in Long Island City, New York, and Toronto, Canada, and glass container plants in Salem, New Jersey, and Connellsville, Pennsylvania.

Anchor Hocking Glass Corporation continued to expand into other areas of production such as tableware, closure and sealing machinery, and toiletries and cosmetic containers through the expansion of existing facilities and the purchase of Baltimore, Maryland, based Carr-Lowry Glass Company and the west coast Maywood Glass. In the 1950s, the corporation established the Research and Development Center in Lancaster, purchased the Tropical Glass and Container Company in Jacksonville, Florida, and built a new facility in San Leandro, California, in 1959.

In 1962, the company built a new glass container plant in Houston, Texas, while also adding a second unit to the Research and Development Center, known as the General Development Laboratory. In 1963, Zanesville Mold Company in Ohio became an Anchor Hocking Corporation subsidiary. The company designed and manufactured mold equipment for Anchor Hocking.

The word "Glass" was dropped from the company's name in 1969 because the company had evolved into an international company with an nearly infinite product list. They had entered the plastic market in 1968 with the acquisition of Plastics Incorporated in St. Paul, Minnesota. They continued to expand their presence in the plastic container market with the construction of a plant in Springdale, Ohio. This plant was designed to produce blown mold plastic containers. Anchor Hocking Corporation entered the lighting field in September 1970 with the purchase of Phoenix Glass Company in Monaca, Pennsyl-vania. They also bought the Taylor, Smith & Taylor Company, located in Chester, West Virginia, to make earthenware, fine stoneware, institutional china dinnerware, and commemorative collector plates.

Over the years, several changes occurred in the company. Phoenix Glass Company was destroyed by fire on 15 July 1978; Shenango China (New Castle, Pennsylvania) was purchased in 28 March 1979; Taylor, Smith & Taylor was sold on 30 September 1981; and on 1 April 1983, the company decided to divest its interest in the Glass Container Division to an affiliate of the Wesray Corporation. The Glass Container Division was to be known as the Anchor Glass Container Corporation with seven manufacturing plants and its office in Lancaster, Ohio.

The Newell Corporation acquired the Anchor Hocking Corporation on 2 July 1987. With this renewed influx of capital, several facilities were upgraded and some less profitable facilities were either closed or sold. The Clarksburg, West Virginia, facility was closed in November 1987, Shenango China was sold on 22 January 1988, and Carr-Lowry Glass was sold on 12 October 1989. Today, Anchor Hocking enjoys the financial backing and resources as one of the eighteen decentralized Newell Companies that manufacture and market products in four basic markets: house wares, hardware, home furnishings, and office products. You may recognize such familiar Newell Companies such as Intercraft, Levolor Home Fashions, Anchor Hocking Glass, Goody Products, Anchor Hocking Specialty Glass, Sanford, Stuart Hall, Newell Home Furnishings, Amerock, BerzOmatic, or Lee/Rowan.

# Identification Marks

Over the years Anchor Hocking has used several identification marks to mark their glassware. In 1980, the company issued a limited edition 75th anniversary ashtray, pictured below, which portrays the corporate identification marks. During the photographing, the marks on the ashtray were blackened with a magic marker so they would show up when photographed. Originally, when the Hocking Glass Company was established in 1905, the company used the mark seen on the left side of the ashtray. This mark was used from 1905 until 1937, when it was replaced by the more familiar anchor over H mark (center of ashtray) to illustrate the merger of the Hocking Glass Company and the Anchor Cap Company. Finally, in October 1977, the company adopted a new symbol (right side of the ashtray), an anchor with a modern, contemporary appearance to further the new corporate identity.

# Catalog Identification

Anchor Hocking used a series of numbers and letters to denote glassware identification in the catalogs. Starting with a basic design number, the company placed a letter (prefix) in front of the number to denote the color and cut or glass type selection. The following is a listing of the letter designations generally used throughout the catalogs:

No prefix - Crystal
E - Forest Green
F - Laser Blue
H - Crystal Fire King
J - Cut Glass
L - Luster Shell
N - Honey Gold
R - Royal Ruby
T - Avocado
Y - Spicy Brown
W - White

For pitchers and glasses, each item of a particular pattern was given its own designation to indicate the capacity. Below are the common capacity designations:

63 - 6 oz. fruit juice
65 - 11 oz. tumbler
69 - 15 oz. iced tea
92 - 19 oz. large iced tea
93 - 22 oz. giant iced tea
3375 - 32 oz. giant sized ice tea
86 - 86 oz. capacity of pitcher

The patterns were also given specific designations. Below is a listing of some common Forest Green pattern designations:

325 - Colonial Lady
351 - Leaf Design
352 - Polka Dots
5612 - Spinning Wheel and Churn
5613 - Wild Geese
5614 - Floral and Diamond
5615 - Gazelle
5705 - Gold and White Vintage
5807 - White Lace

Putting this all together, the #E92/5612 would indicate a Forest Green tumbler (E), 19 oz. large iced tea (92), in the Spinning Wheel and Churn pattern (5612).

---

# What is Glass?

Most people were taught that there are three states of matter in the universe: solids, liquids, and gasses. So, how would you classify glass? People, who have hit a car window during an automobile accident or leaned on a glass counter in a department store would say that glass is a solid. Well, that is not the case. A solid, by definition, is any material that retains its shape without being contained. Glass is constantly flowing and does not retain it shape. Now, the process is extremely slow. Glass is termed a super cooled liquid because it is solid and molecular motion only ceases when glass is at −459.69 degrees Fahrenheit (absolute zero). At this temperature, which has never been achieved, glass would become a solid. If a substance was a solid, it should have a melting point. There are no melting points listed for glass since it is always a liquid except at absolute zero. When companies process glass, they are not melting the glass; they are only making it more fluid. The hotter the glass gets, the more fluid it becomes.

Have you ever noticed that old glass windows tend to rattle as they get older? They also are wavy in appearance. How does this happen and why are the lines in a window always horizontal? First, since glass is a super cooled liquid that is always in motion, it is being constantly pulled downward by gravity. The process is very, very slow. Over a number of years, the glass begins to form irregular wavy lines on the surface. The top of a pane of glass is becoming thinner and the bottom becoming thicker. Eventually, the glass at the top of the windowpane becomes so thin that it is loose in the frame. Any loud noise, gust of wind or strong movement within the building will cause the top of the windowpane to move and rattle.

Now consider what happens when someone hits a baseball through that old window. After the ball has shattered the windowpane, the top pieces fall out easily. But the bottom pieces remain firmly affixed in the window frame. Over the years, as gravity pulled the glass downward, the thickness of the windowpane was increasing at the bottom edge. This wedged the glass between the putty and window frame. Even with the ball rocketing through the window, the lower portion of the window remained firmly in place while the top pieces fell out of the frame. Even in the horror movies you see people injured by the glass falling out of the top of the frame while the bottom pieces remain firmly in place. They are not using old windows, they just happen to be recreating what would really happen when an old window is broken.

# Fire King Glass Versus Regular Glass

Confusion exists over the differences between Fire King and regular soda lime glass. Fire King is not a brand name for glass, it is a type of glass. Fire King is borosilicate glass made by melting a combination of sand with sodium borate. This glass melts at a temperature about 200 degrees Fahrenheit higher than regular soda lime glass. Borosilicate glass is noted for its very low expansion coefficient. It can be used in ovens for cooking, but not on the stove. During the making of Fire King glass, the furnace emits boron compounds that are environmentally "unfriendly" and corrosive to the brick lining in the glass furnaces. For these reasons, Fire King glass is reasonable expensive to produce.

What we know as "regular" glass is a melted mixture of sand, soda ash (anhydrous sodium carbonate), and limestone (calcium carbonate). It has an expansion rate three times that of borosilicate glass. When heated unevenly (i.e., on a stove), the heated portions near the hot stove elements will expand at three times the rate of the unheated portions. This will cause internal stress points to form in the glass. If the stress becomes sufficient, cracking will occur.

---

# Anchor Hocking Glass Museum

Since I started collecting Anchor Hocking glass I have always heard and read about the infamous "morgue." The "morgue" is located at Anchor Hocking's Lancaster, Ohio, plant. The "morgue" contains examples of glass production spanning many years. I have toured the area on more than one occasion and found it to be very interesting. Access to the "morgue" is severely limited because the area is located in the middle of the production facility. The majority of the pieces of glass in the "morgue" are later production pieces and generally only cover production at the Lancaster, Ohio, plant. The glass is displayed on large shelves on rollers. The glass is crowded, unlabelled, not well organized, and very difficult to observe because the roller shelves can only be separated by about three to four feet. I did not see examples of Anchor Hocking's bottle production, but there are examples of glass produced in other divisions of the company. Overall, it was an interesting piece of Anchor Hocking history to see and an exciting experience.

I think it is important for everyone to actually see the glass that Anchor Hocking produced, so I am building a facility to display my collection of over 8,000 pieces of Anchor Hocking glass. With a couple of exceptions, all the glass pictured in my books will be on display in the museum. There will also be some unknown pieces of Anchor Hocking glass on display that will be featured in upcoming books. The museum will not have regular hours of operation. The collection can be viewed by calling the museum on a phone number that will be published once the museum is officially open. I designed and built the facility over the last 18 months and included a long porch that will have rocking chairs for visitors to sit in and relax. We are already planning a second facility to display an extensive collection of boxed sets, more glass, and company catalogs. Eventually, we will also add a photo studio to the facility.

This is the catalog page listing the plain Finlandia style pitcher. The catalogs list Finlandia in Laser Blue, Crystal, Honey Gold, Aquamarine, and Avocado Green.

The same catalog also lists the decorated Finlandia style pitcher with floral decorations as Misty Daisy. The Misty Daisy decoration was applied to all the colors of the plain Finlandia design pitcher.

Common stock certificate for the Anchor Cap Corporation.

Common stock certificate for the Anchor Cap Corporation.

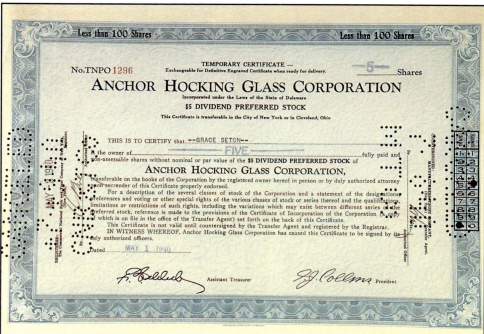

Common stock certificate for the Anchor Hocking Glass Corporation.

The three identification marks used by the company.

The 75th anniversary ashtray in the original box, $50-55.

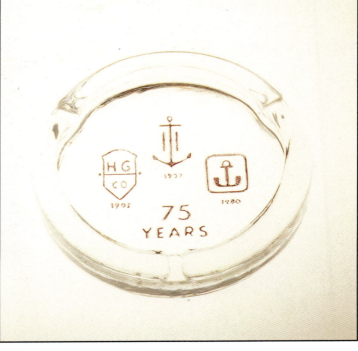

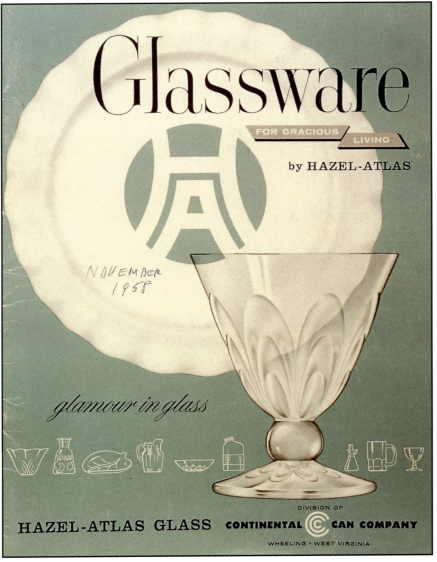

Glassware
FOR GRACIOUS LIVING
by HAZEL-ATLAS

NOVEMBER 1958

glamour in glass

HAZEL-ATLAS GLASS  CONTINENTAL CAN COMPANY

DIVISION OF

WHEELING · WEST VIRGINIA

The mark of the Hazel Atlas Glass Company is often confused as being a mark for Anchor Hocking Glass Company. If this were the mark for Anchor Hocking, the letters would be reversed with the capital "A" over the lower case "h".

# CHAPTER ONE
# Simple Methods to Identify Anchor Hocking Pitchers

There are some very simple ways to distinguish Anchor Hocking pitchers from those of other glass companies. Most of the pitchers in this book were identified from the extensive library of company catalogs that I have. When the particular pitcher cannot be located in the catalogs, I use another method. While the companies did tend to copy decorations applied to the glass, there are some very pronounced differences in the shape or design of the pitcher itself.

Left to right: Bartlett-Collins Satin finish 80 oz. ice lip jug pitcher; Anchor Hocking Finlandia design pitcher. While both of the pitchers are similar in height, there are two distinct differences. First, the Bartlett-Collins pitcher is flat on the bottom while the Anchor Hocking Finlandia design pitcher has a 3/8" pedestal. Second, the Bartlett-Collins pitcher's sides spread out more near the base, while the Anchor Hocking Finlandia pitcher's sides are more vertical.

Left to right: Anchor Hocking 86 oz. upright pitcher; Bartlett-Collins 80 oz. ice lip jug Decoration #103 made in 1955. You will notice that the sides of the Anchor Hocking pitcher are more curved than the Bartlett-Collins pitcher. Also, the shoulder of the Anchor Hocking pitcher has a distinct series of flat spots while the Bartlett-Collins pitcher shoulder is smooth.

Left to right: Bartlett-Collins #100 ball jug Decoration #18 made in 1942; Anchor Hocking tilt ball pitcher; Bartlett-Collins #100 ball jug Decoration #377 made from 1938 to 1940. There are three distinct differences between the pitchers from the two companies. First, the Anchor Hocking tilt ball pitcher has circular rings around the neck. These rings are not found on Bartlett-Collins ball jugs. Second, the handle of an Anchor Hocking pitcher curves farther away from the pitcher. Finally, the neck of the Anchor Hocking pitcher is about 50 percent taller than Bartlett-Collins pitchers.

Left to right: Anchor Hocking 86 oz. upright pitcher; Hazel Atlas 80 oz. jug number 52X-1816 decoration #1033 made from 1938 to 1939. You will notice that the Hazel Atlas pitcher is about 3/4" taller than the Anchor Hocking pitcher, it is thinner in diameter, and the shoulder has a totally different shape.

Many collectors confuse Anchor Hocking and Hazel Atlas pitchers, especially these two. The most noticeable difference is the multiple lines that circle around the neck, shoulder area, and base of the Hazel Atlas pitcher. Anchor Hocking pitchers were not made with this multiple line design.

Hazel Atlas beverage sets were even packed in boxes similar to Anchor Hocking's boxes.

Close-up of the multiple lines that circle the neck and shoulder area of many Hazel Atlas pitchers.

Left to right: Anchor Hocking 86 oz. upright pitcher; Federal #175 85 oz. decoration #8580 South Seas pitcher made in 1953. There are two basic differences to look for here. First, the handle of the Federal pitcher is horizontal at the top, while the Anchor Hocking pitcher's handle is completely curved from top to bottom. Second, the sides of the Federal pitcher are more curved so the base is smaller in diameter than the Anchor Hocking pitcher.

Left to right: Anchor Hocking 86 oz. upright pitcher; Federal #177 85 oz. decoration #7890 Windows pitcher made in 1963. There are four distinct differences to observe. First, the handle of the Federal pitcher is horizontal at the top. Second, there is a distinct line around the shoulder of the Federal pitcher. Third, the base of the Federal pitcher has a ½" pedestal. Finally, the sides of the Federal pitcher are basically straight while the Anchor Hocking pitcher's sides are gently curved.

The Federal Windows decoration beverage set in the original box.

Left to right: Federal 32 oz. juice pitcher; Anchor Hocking 36 oz. juice pitcher; Federal 32 oz. juice pitcher. While both the Federal and Anchor Hocking juice pitchers have the same general shape and height, there are two distinct differences. First, the upper portion of the Anchor Hocking pitcher's handle is horizontal while the Federal pitcher's handle is completely curved from top to bottom. Second, the Federal pitcher has a smaller diameter than the Anchor Hocking pitcher.

Since most Anchor Hocking and Libbey pitchers are almost impossible to tell apart, boxed sets become increasingly important in identification. The yellow frosted pitcher looks identical to the Anchor Hocking 86 oz. upright pitcher. Unless you found the frosted pitcher in the original box you might not know who made it. Since Libbey and Anchor Hocking pitchers and glasses are so similar, be sure to look at the glasses for clues. Most Libbey glasses have an upper case cursive "L" in the glass. Most of the Libbey gold designed glasses are marked with this symbol. The same holds true with most Hazel Atlas sets. While the pitchers are not generally marked, the glasses usually have the upper case "H" over the lower case "a" mark.

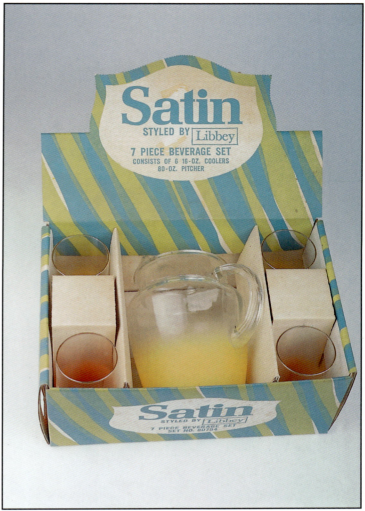

Left to right: Libbey 32 oz. juice pitcher; Anchor Hocking 36 oz. juice pitcher. Notice that the horizontal area of the handle is on the bottom of the Libbey pitcher but on the top of the Anchor Hocking pitcher. The Libbey pitcher also has a smaller diameter.

Left to right: Anchor Hocking 86 oz. upright pitcher; Libbey 86 oz. upright pitcher. Notice the pitchers are virtually identical with the exception of the applied yellow decoration.

19

Boxed set of Line Lites. These sets are being sold on the internet as Anchor Hocking products when, in fact, they are not. Anchor Glass Container made these glasses. This is not an Anchor Hocking company. Anchor Glass Container also uses a mark that looks like two "Js" placed back to back. This symbol is mistaken for the Anchor Hocking "anchor over H" symbol used from 1937 to 1977.

Close-up of label on the Line Lites box.

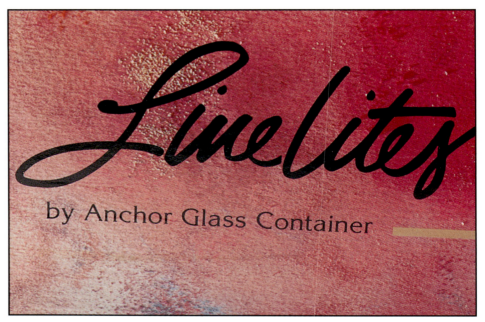

Another set of glasses sold by Anchor Glass Container.

Through the years I have been amazed at the combinations of pitchers and glasses that I have discovered. With the advent of companies such as Gay Fad Studio of Lancaster, Ohio, pitchers and glasses from different companies were "married" together to produce some unusual combinations. The Gay Fad Studio hand-painted glassware from several companies and either they, or some other company, sold glass from different companies as sets. Below are some unusual examples.

Macbeth-Evans Corning 80 oz. hand made ice lip chiller with marked 11 oz. 4 ¾" Anchor Hocking straight shell glasses, $75-85 for the entire set.

Marked Anchor Hocking 40 oz. chiller with marked Federal Glass Company 3 ½" glasses, $40-50 for the entire set.

Bartlett-Collins yellow frosted 80 oz. ice lip jug with Anchor Hocking 9 oz. 4 7/8" coupette glasses, $30-40 for the entire set.

Two very similar designs for the 9 oz. coupette glasses. Left to right: Anchor Hocking coupette, $2-5; Bartlett-Collins coupette, $2-5.

Notice the small "wafer" of glass just under the bowl of the coupette on the left. This is common on Anchor Hocking stemmed glasses. The Bartlett-Collins coupette on the right does not have the wafer.

Mountaineer Glass etched pitcher with Anchor Hocking 5 oz. 3 3/8" Roly Poly juice glasses, $40-50 for the entire set.

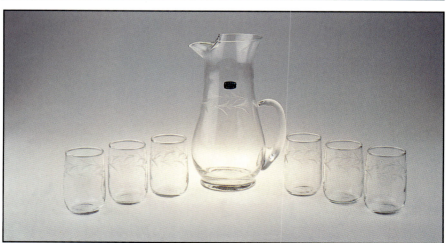

Bartlett-Collins ice lip pitcher with marked Anchor Hocking 5 oz. 3 3/8" Roly Poly juice glasses, $50-60 for the entire set. The glasses are marked with the "anchor over H" emblem.

Marked Federal 6 ½" (to the top of the spout) cocktail shaker with Anchor Hocking 3 ½ oz. 3" cocktail glasses.

This was not the only "mix and match" process going on during these years. Even Anchor Hocking mixed patterns to produce some unusual sets. Above is a Finlandia style pitcher that is covered with the Pagoda design surface. The set was not sold with Finlandia style glasses, but sold with Pagoda water glasses.

# CHAPTER THREE

# Not All Hand-Painted
# Glass Was Made by the Gay Fad Studio

This photo was supposed to have been taken in the Gay Fad Studio. Notice all the different decorations and types of glass sold by the studio.

Over the years collectors have come to treasure hand-painted glassware. Probably the most notable company to hand-paint glass was the Gay Fad Studio of Lancaster, Ohio. When most collectors see hand-painted items, they naturally conclude the glass was painted at the Gay Fad Studio. Unfortunately, this is not always true. There were many art studios besides the Gay Fad Studio that hand-painted glassware. I have found pieces of glass with labels from Hansetta-Artware Company of New York, New York, Washington Company of Washington, Pennsylvania, United Glass Industries (location unknown), and Imperial (location unknown). Information about these art studios and companies is very limited due to their small size, brief history, and limited production. Undoubtedly, there are others that will surface in time.

While most people associate the Gay Fad Studio with hand-painted glassware, the studio was also responsible for producing many machine-decorated items. Many of the decorations are so intricate that they could only have been done by machine.

Hansetta-Artware Company hand-painted pitcher and glasses. The set consisted of a Federal 85 oz. pitcher and six Anchor Hocking 3 ½ oz. 3" cocktail glasses, $75-100 for the set with label.

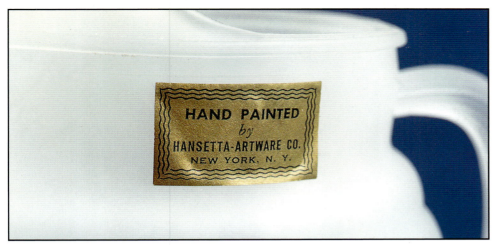

Close-up of the Hansetta-Artware Company label.

Hansetta-Artware Company hand-painted pitcher and glasses. The set consisted of an Anchor Hocking 40 oz. juice pitcher and six Baltic 5 oz. 3 ¾" juice glasses, $75-100 for the set with the label.

Hansetta-Artware Company hand-painted pitcher and glasses. The set consisted of a Federal 85 oz. ice lip pitcher with six Anchor Hocking 11 oz. 4 ¾" straight shell glasses, $75-100 for the set with the label.

Photo of Gay Fad Studio machine decorated pitcher and glasses. The set consisted of an Anchor Hocking 86 oz. upright pitcher with the 15 oz. 5 ¼" straight shell glasses, $75-85 for the set with the Gay Fad marking.

Close-up of the Gay Fad signature on the pitcher.

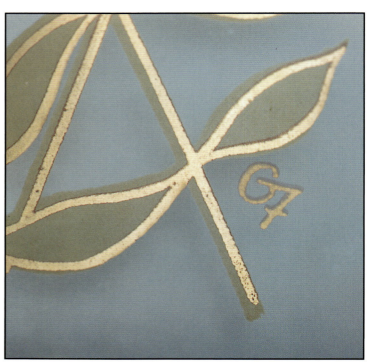

The Gay Fad marking on the juice pitcher was only the "GF" initials.

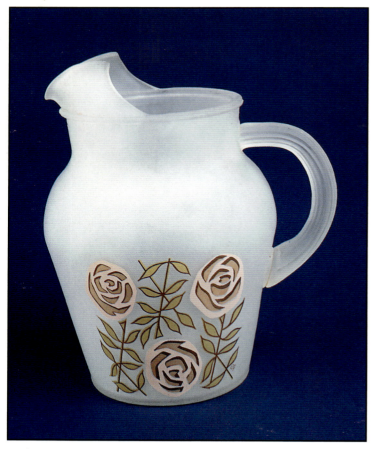

Photo of 40 oz. juice pitcher with the same design as the 86 oz. upright pitcher, $25-35 for the pitcher alone.

Box containing a Gay Fad 7-Piece Juice Set, $80-100 for the complete set, $25-30 for the box only.

The 7-Piece Juice Set removed from the box. The set consisted of a Federal 36 oz. juice jug #2604 with six 3" glasses with machine applied designs, $60-70 for the set without the box.

*Center right:* Another 7-Piece Beverage Set sold by Gay Fad Studio, $100-125 for the complete set, $25-30 for the box only.

*Center left:* Photo of a Christmas glass from Gay Fad Studio. The design was applied by machine to a Hazel Atlas 3" glass, $5-7.

The 7-Piece Beverage Set was hand-painted by United Glass Industries, yet it was sold in a box marked with Gay Fad Studio. The set consisted of one 86 oz. pitcher and six 10 oz. 5" tapered glasses, $80-100 for the set without the box.

Photo of United Glass Industries hand-painted pitcher and glasses. The set consisted of the Anchor Hocking 36 oz. juice pitcher with six Anchor Hocking 5 oz. 3 3/8" Roly Poly fruit juice glasses, $80-100 for the set with the label.

Photo of United Glass Industries hand-painted pitcher and glasses with the butterfly design. The set consisted of an Anchor Hocking 36 oz. juice pitcher with six Anchor Hocking 6 oz. 3 ¾" juice glasses, $80-100 for the set with the label.

Boxed Beverage Set made by Washington Company of Washington, Pennsylvania, $100-125 for the complete set with the box, $30-35 for the box only. The Washington Company did hand-paint and color treat glassware from many different companies, but mainly Hazel Atlas. Some of the more common pieces were pitcher sets, salad sets, and serving pieces. The company employed about a dozen women as artists. Like the Gay Fad Studio, they did not produce any glassware. The company was located near the Hazel Atlas plant number 1. The Washington Company was in business from the late 1940s until the late 1960s and they may have been a subsidiary of Hazel Atlas, although as of this writing that association remains unclear.

The 7-Piece Beverage Set consisted of one Anchor Hocking 86 oz. upright pitcher and six 10 oz. 5" tapered glasses, $80-100 for the set with the label.

*Left:* Close-up of the Washington Company label.

*Right:* This hand-painted Royal Ruby ivy ball brings up an interesting point. There may be yet another company that hand-painted pitchers and glasses, as well as Royal Ruby items. This is the only piece of glass I have found with this label. If you have any information about the company, please contact me.

29

# CHAPTER FOUR
# Cracking in Anchor Hocking Pitchers

You may have noticed that Anchor Hocking pitchers, especially the pitchers made prior to 1970, may have cracks at the base of the handles. When glass cools in an open environment (not in a controlled furnace or lehr), it has a tendency to cool unevenly. The thicker portions of the pitcher (i.e., the handle) retain the heat longer. This uneven cooling may cause stress points to form in the glass. The stress can only be relieved in two ways. You can reheat the pitcher and control and extend the cooling process to eliminate the stress points. If that was not done, glass will inherently relieve the stress points through the second method of stress relief . . . cracking. Most of the pitchers produced by Anchor Hocking were allowed to air cool, thereby promoting uneven cooling and some handle cracking. Since many of the cracks are very difficult to see unless viewed under strong illumination, cracked pitchers may have been sold to the public by mistake. The cracks did not affect the use of the pitcher since many of the pitchers were used for over 50 years without the handle falling off or the pitcher leaking.

Cracked handle on Tree of Life design pitcher produced in 1933.

Cracked handle on Swirl design tilt ball pitcher produced in the 1950s.

Cracked handle on a Lido (Milano) design Laser Blue pitcher produced in the 1970s. With the darker colored pitchers, the cracks may be very difficult to see.

# CHAPTER FIVE

# 86 Ounce Pitchers

Left to right: Large Red Flower decoration pitcher #86/353 (1952 to 1954), $20-25; Diamond and Flower decoration pitcher #86/281 (1957 to 1958), $20-25; Stereo Waves decoration pitcher #86/6005 (1959 to 1960), $20-25.

Left to right: Riviera decoration #92/359 19 oz. large iced tea, 6 7/8", $10-12; Riviera decoration pitcher #86/359 pitcher (1954), $20-25; Red Leaves and Wavy Lines decoration pitcher #86/5811 (1957 to 1958), $20-25; 11 oz. tumbler #65/5811, 4 ¾", $5-10.

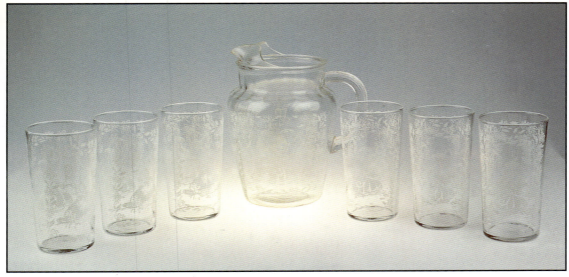

Colonial Lady decoration #86/325 pitcher, $20-25, with six #69/325 15 oz. iced teas, 6", $8-10 for each glass.

Confetti decoration pitcher #86/5709 (1957 to 1958), $20-25, with four #65/5709 11 oz. tumblers, 4 ¾", $5-10 for each glass.

Red Rose decoration pitcher #86/5804 (1957 to 1958), $20-25 with six #65/5804 11 oz. tumblers, 4 ¾", $5-10 for each glass.

Ming Tree decoration pitcher #86/6204 (1962 to 1963), $20-25.

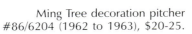

Curlicue decoration pitcher #86/6205 (1962 to 1963), $20-25, with six #65/6205 11 oz. tumblers, 4 ¾", $5-10 for each glass.

Left to right: Tulip Garden decoration #86/5907 pitcher (1958 to 1960), $20-25; Pink Aster decoration pitcher #86/5616 (1956 to 1957), $20-25; Yellow Dogwood decoration pitcher #86/393 (1955), $20-25.

Balloons decoration pitcher #86/6006 (1960), $20-25, with six #65/6006 11 oz. tumblers, 4 ¾", $5-10 for each glass.

Balloons decoration four-pack of #69/6006 15 oz. iced tea glasses, $20-30.

Royale Blue decoration pitcher #86/6118 (1961-1962), $25-30, with four #3732/6118 12 oz. tumblers, 5 5/8", $10-15 for each glass, and two #3602/6118 4 oz. cocktails, 2 ¾", $8-10 for each glass. This pattern was listed in the *Family Stamps Gift Book* from the Family Stamp Company of Cleveland, Ohio. In the catalog, the pattern is listed as Gold and Blue Lustre design. You could get a set of either eight 9 oz. or eight 12 oz. tumblers for only one book of stamps.

Coral Tulip decoration pitcher #86/371 (1955), $20-25, with six #69/371 15 oz. iced tea glasses, 6", $8-10 for each glass.

Contemporary decoration pitcher #86/5707 (1956 to 1957), $20-25, with six #65/5707 11 oz. tumblers, 4 ¾", $8-10 for each glass.

Pink Raffia decoration pitcher #86/5913 (1958 to 1959), $20-25, with four #92/5913 19 oz. large iced teas, 6", $8-10 for each glass.

Floral and Diamond decoration pitcher #86/5604 (1956 to 1957), $20-25, with six #65/5604 11 oz. tumblers, 4 ¾", $5-10 for each glass.

Triangles decoration pitcher #86/5619 (1956 to 1957), $20-25, with six #69/5619 15 oz. iced teas, 6", $5-10 for each glass.

Contempo decoration pitcher #86/322 (1958 to 1959), $20-25, with six #65/322 11 oz. tumblers, 4 ¾", $5-10 for each glass.

Antiques decoration pitcher #86/6305 (1962 to 1963), $20-25, with two #69/6305 15 oz. iced teas, 6", $5-10 for each glass.

Rose and Wavy Lines decoration pitcher #86/5618 (1956 to 1957), $20-25, with six #69/5618 15 oz. iced teas, 6", $5-10 for each glass.

Rose and Wavy Lines decoration tumblers. Left to right: 15 oz. iced tea #69/5618, 6", $5-10; 11 oz. tumbler #65/5618, 4 ¾", $5-10; 6 oz. fruit juice #63/5618, 3 ¾", $5-8.

The Rose and Wavy Lines decoration pitcher was produced in two color versions, $20-25 for each color.

Weather Vane decoration pitcher #86/6304 (1962 to 1963), $20-25, with six #66/6304 11 ½ oz. tumblers, 4 ¾", $5-10 for each glass. There is also an orange and yellow version of this pattern (not shown).

Pastel Bands decoration pitcher #86/6203 (1961 to 1962), $20-25, with six #69/6203 15 oz. iced teas, 6", $5-10 for each glass.

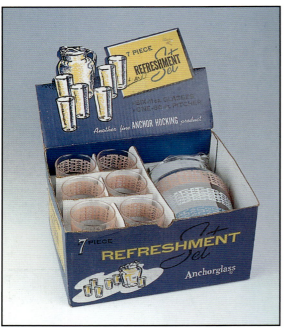

Boxed refreshment set of Pastel Bands decoration glassware, $50-75 for the entire set with the box, $10-15 for the box only.

Pastel Bands decoration glasses. Left to right: 32 oz. giant iced tea #3375/6203, 7", $15-20; 15 oz. iced tea #69/6203, 6", $5-10; 11 oz. tumbler #65/6203, 4 ¾", $5-10; 6 oz. fruit juice #63/6203, 3 ¾", $5-8.

White Roses and Gold Wreath decoration pitcher #86/5801 (1959), $20-25, with six #65/5801 11 oz. tumblers, 4 ¾", $5-10 for each glass.

Mosaic decoration pitcher #86/6424 (1964), $20-25, with six 16 oz. iced teas, 6 ½", $5-10 for each glass. There are three colored versions of the glasses: #3526/6422 with white, light green, blue, and green squares; #3526/6423 with white, light green, coral, and purple squares; #3526/6424 with white, light green, yellow, and orange squares.

Alpine decoration pitcher #86/6403 (1964), $20-25, with six #66/6403 11 ½ oz. tumblers, 4 7/8", $5-10 for each glass.

There were six sizes of glasses made with the Alpine decoration, although only two are shown here. Left to right: 11 ½ oz. tumbler #66/6403, 4 7/8", $5-10; 9 ½ oz. tumbler #3519/6403, 4 ¾", $5-10.

Left to right: White Roses and Gold Wreath decoration 19 oz. large iced tea #92/5801, 6 ¼", $8-10; 11 oz. tumbler #65/5801, 4 ¾", $5-10.

39

Golden Peaks decoration pitcher #86/6419 (1964), $25-30, with four #3735/6419 14 oz. coolers, 6 5/8", $8-10 for each glass.

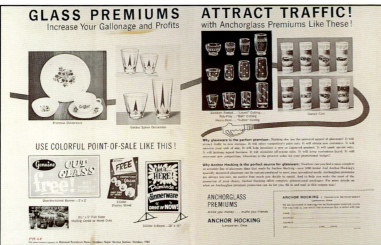

Rare advertising proof showing another name for the Golden Peaks decoration. Here the decoration is called Golden Spikes and this premium advertisement appeared in the October 1961 issues of both the *National Petroleum News* and *Super Service Station.*

Daisy Lace decoration pitcher #86/6801 (1970), $20-25, with six #69/6801 16 oz. beverage glasses, 6", $5-10 for each glass.

Dutch Country decoration pitcher #86/5902 (1958 to 1959), $20-25, with two #69/5902 15 oz. iced tea glasses, 6", $5-10 for each glass.

The three pitchers shown here have the same basic decoration with different color variations. The first color version produced was the pitcher on the left. This is the Bermuda decoration pitcher #86/6703 (1968). Shortly after the Bermuda decoration was introduced, the colors were modified to produce the pitcher on the left, the Kinetic decoration pitcher #86/7104 (1971). The plain yellow version in the middle is the Moire decoration pitcher #86/6608.

Wrought Iron decoration pitcher #86/5607 (1957 to 1958), $50-75, with six #65/5607 11 oz. tumblers, 4 ¾", $10-15 for each glass.

Left to right: Wrought Iron decoration pitcher #86/5805 (1957 to 1958), $20-25; Wrought Iron decoration pitcher #86/5607 (1957 to 1958), $40-50. It is interesting that Anchor Hocking produced two different pitchers with the same decoration name in the same year.

Wrought Iron decoration glasses. Left to right: 19 oz. large iced tea #62/5607, 6 ½", $15-20; 11 oz. tumbler #65/5607, 4 ¾", $10-15; 6 oz. fruit juice #63/5607, 3 ¾", $10-12.

Wrought Iron decoration 40 oz. juice chiller #283/5607, $80-100, with four #63/5607 6 oz. fruit juice glasses, 3 ¾", $10-12 for each glass.

Two Wrought Iron four-packs of 11 oz. tumblers #65/5607, $60-75 for each four-pack.

The Park Lane decoration 11 oz. tumbler, 4 ¾", $5-10 for each glass. This is the yellow version and there may be a matching pitcher.

Left to right: Park Lane decoration pitcher #86/6105 (1961), $20-25; 6 oz. fruit juice #63/6105, 3 ¾", $5-10 for each glass.

Left to right: Chantilly Lace decoration pitcher #86/5909 (1959), $20-25; Outdoorsman decoration pitcher with black ducks, ring-necked pheasants, and bobwhite quail, $20-25; Modern Blocks decoration pitcher #86/5706 (1957 to 1958), $20-25.

Left to right: Colored Triangles decoration pitcher #86/5814 (1957 to 1958), $20-25; Colonial Kitchen decoration pitcher #86/6003 (1959 to 1960), $20-25; Medallion decoration pitcher #86/5911 (1959), $20-25.

Left to right: Balloons Away decoration pitcher #86/6411 (1964), $20-25; Red Rose decoration pitcher #86/373 (1955), $20-25; Fleur-De-Lis decoration pitcher #86/6029 (1959 to 1960), $20-25.

Left to right: White Leaves and Gold Grecian Keys decoration pitcher #86/378 (1957 to 1958), $20-25; Strawberry Patch decoration pitcher #86/7103 (1971), $20-25; Filigree decoration pitcher #86/6212 (1962 to 1963), $20-25.

English Flower decoration pitcher #86/377 (1955), $20-25, with six #65/377 11 oz. tumblers, 4 ¾", $10-12 for each glass.

Pastel Stripes decoration glassware includes one 86 oz. pitcher #86/6404 (1964), $20-30, four #66/6404 11 ½ oz. 4 ¾" tumblers, $4-5 each, and one 40 oz. juice chiller #3440/6404, $25-30.

Fiesta Bands decoration pitcher #86/6201 (1964), $20-25, with six #66/6201 11 ½ oz. tumblers, 4 ¾", $5-8 for each glass.

Rare Forest Green pitcher with ash leaf decoration, $75-80. A similar decoration called September Gold (applied to the Honey Gold Finlandia glasses and Chateau design pitcher) and September Blue (applied to the Laser Blue Finlandia glasses and Chateau design pitcher) were both listed in the 1974 catalog.

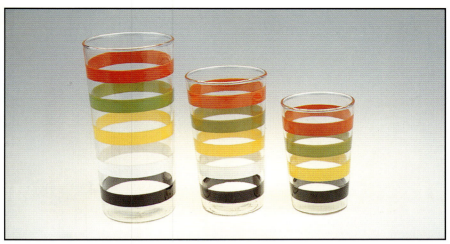

Fiesta Bands decoration tumblers. Left to right: 15 oz. iced tea #69/6201 (1964), 6", $8-10; 11 ½ oz. tumbler #66/6201, 4 ¾", $5-8; 6 oz. juice #63/6201, 3 ¾", $4-5.

Green and Black Saloon Stripes decoration pitcher #86/7018 (1970), $25-30, with four #3526-C/7016 16 oz. beverage glasses, 6 ½", $5-8 for each glass.

Silver Laurel etched 86 oz. pitcher #J86/100 (1970) with four #J3170/100 10 ½ oz. heavy base tumblers, 5", $4-5 for each glass.

Wide Bands decoration pitcher #86/5624 (1955), $25-30, with the #3658/5624 13 oz. iced tea, 5", $5-8 for each glass.

Fiesta Bands decoration pitcher #86/39 (1957 to 1958), $25-30 with four #65/39 11 oz. tumblers, 4 ¾", $5-8 for each glass.

Left to right: 32 oz. giant iced tea #3375/39, 6 ⅞", $15-20; 11 oz. tumbler #65/39, 4 ¾", $5-8.

White and Frosted Snowflake decoration 86 oz. pitcher #86/5923 (1961), $20-30, with six #3526/5923 16 oz. iced teas, 6 ½", $3-4 for each glass. When this decoration was first produced, the snowflakes were all white. In 1967 the decoration was again produced but with two modifications. First, the name was changed to just Snowflake and second, the colors in the diamonds near the rim of the glass were also added to the center of the snowflake decorations.

There are two versions of each glass. Notice that the snowflake is either all white (produced in 1961) or white with a colored center matching the color of the diamonds on the rim of the glass (produced in 1967), $3-4 for any of the glasses. The 1967 catalog only lists the black, blue, and pink glasses with the colored snowflakes.

The catalogs only list four colors of the diamonds on the rim of the glasses: blue, black, pink, and green. Here are at least two more colors. I have also seen the glasses with yellow diamonds.

White and Satin Swirl decoration 16 oz. iced tea #3526/6123 (1961), 6 ½", $5-6 for each glass. The decoration is also available in black, blue, and green swirl colors. There is also a matching 86 oz. pitcher.

The glasses with the 22 kt. gold diamonds were not listed in the catalogs. This 22 kt. gold diamond version may have been a special edition given away as a premium, $8-10 for each glass. The ice bucket was also not listed in the catalogs, $30-40.

Two versions of the Candy Stripe decoration 86 oz. pitcher. Left to right: Flame Red and White Candy Stripe 86 oz. pitcher #86/406 (1954), $25-30; another Candy Stripe decoration 86 oz. pitcher, $25-30.

Horse and Buggy decoration 86 oz. pitcher #86/6202 (1961 to 1962), $25-30, with six #69/6202 15 oz. iced teas, 6", $5-8 for each glass.

Left to right: 19 oz. large iced tea #92/6202, 6 ¼", $8-10; 15 oz. iced tea #69/6202, 6", $5-8; 11 oz. tumbler #65/6202, 5", $5-8; 6 oz. fruit juice #63/6202, 3 ¾", $4-5; 11 oz. tumbler in yellow and white, $10-12. There may be a matching pitcher for the yellow and white version of the Horse and Buggy decoration.

Four-pack of Horse and Buggy decoration glasses, $20-30.

Sailing Boats decoration 86 oz. pitcher #86/5603 (1956), $40-50, with six #65/5603 11 oz. tumblers, 4 ¾", $8-10 for each glass.

Colonial Days decoration glassware (1968). Left to right: 86 oz. pitcher #86/6501, $25-30; 19 oz. large iced tea #92/6501, 6 ¼", $5-8; 16 oz. iced tea #69/6501, 6", $5-8; 11 ½ oz. tumbler #66/6501, 4 ¾", $4-5; 6 oz. fruit juice #63/6501, 3 ½", $3-5.

The 22 kt. gold decoration on Anchor Hocking glassware is easily removed when tape is applied over the decoration and then peeled off. Here is what happened when the tape holding a price tag was removed.

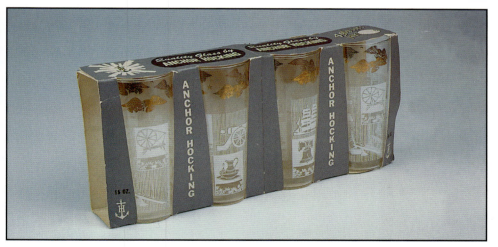

Four-pack of unidentified Anchor Hocking glasses, $20-25.

Left to right: 86 oz. pitcher with frosted and 22 kt. gold decorations, $25-30; 86 oz. pitcher with white leaves and lines, $25-30; 86 oz. pitcher with a decoration similar to Wrought Iron, $25-30.

Circus decoration 86 oz. pitcher #86/7100 (1971), $25-30, with four #69/7100 16 oz. iced teas, 5", $5-8 for each glass.

There are three versions of the frosted Fiesta Bands decoration that may have pitchers to match, $5-8 for each glass.

Left to right: another version of the Fiesta Stripes decoration 86 oz. pitcher, $25-30; Three Wide Bands decoration 86 oz. pitcher #86/137 (1954), $25-30.

Frosted Fiesta Bands decoration 86 oz. pitcher, $30-35, with four 15 oz. glasses, 6 ½", $5-8 for each glass.

Navajo decoration 86 oz. pitcher #86/6902 (1969), $20-25.

Carousel decoration glassware (1968). Left to right: 40 oz. chiller #3340/6803, $20-25; 86 oz. pitcher #86/6803, $25-30; 6 oz. juice #63/6803, 3 ¾", $3-5.

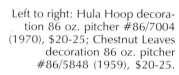

Left to right: Hula Hoop decoration 86 oz. pitcher #86/7004 (1970), $20-25; Chestnut Leaves decoration 86 oz. pitcher #86/5848 (1959), $20-25.

Left to right: Harmony decoration 86 oz. pitcher #86/6207 (1962 to 1963), $20-25; 4-pack of #69/6207 15 oz. iced teas, 5", $20-25.

Left to right; Pastel Ribbons decoration 86 oz. pitcher #86/6007, $25-30; 32 oz. giant iced tea #3375/6007, 6 ¾", $15-20.

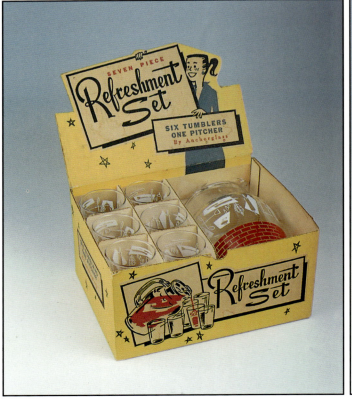

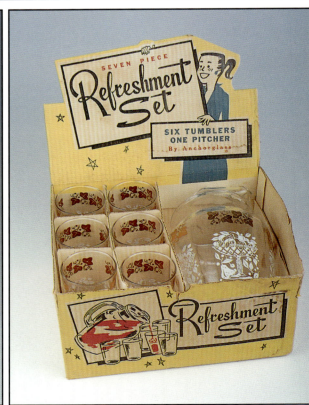

*Left:* Colonial Kitchen decoration 7-Piece Refreshment Set containing one 86 oz. pitcher #86/6003, $20-25, and six #65/6003 11 oz. tumblers, $3-5 for each glass, $10-15 for the box only. Right: White Fruit and Leaves 7-Piece Refreshment Set containing one 86 oz. pitcher #86/6001, $20-25, and six #65/6001 11 oz. tumblers, $3-5 for each glass, $10-15 for the box only.

Pinot Blanc
decoration 86 oz.
pitcher #86/7003
(1970), $30-35,
with six #66/7003
11 ½ oz. tumblers,
5", $5-8 for each
tumbler.

Ball Cutting (Cut
#121) on a 86 oz.
pitcher #86/121
(1961), $30-40,
with six 15 oz.
tumblers, 6", $4-5
for each tumbler.

Creole Rose
decoration
#69/5910 15 oz.
iced tea (1959 to
1960), 6", $3-4 for
each glass. There is
a matching 86 oz.
pitcher with this
decoration.

*Top:* The four-packs are marked by Anchor Hocking, $20-30 for each size. I have not been able to identify the pattern on the pitcher, $20-30.

*Center:* Foreign Language Tiger tumblers and matching pitcher given away at ESSO gas stations, $40-50 for the pitcher and $3-4 for each 5 ½" heavy based tumbler.

Yellow Rose decoration tumblers (1961). Left to right: 11 oz. tumbler #65/6108, 4 ¾", $3-4; 6 oz. fruit juice #63/6108, 3 ¾", $2-3. There is also a matching 86 oz. pitcher with this decoration.

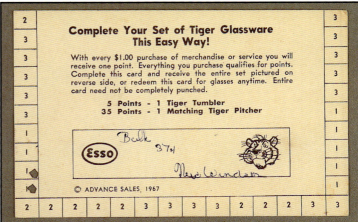

ESSO giveaway card for the Tiger tumblers and matching pitcher (1967), $30-40 for the card.

Backside of the giveaway card for the Tiger tumblers and matching pitcher.

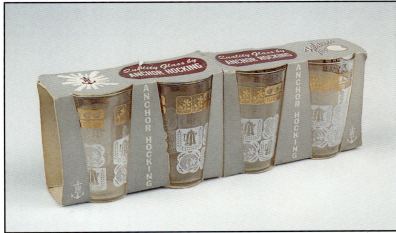

Four-pack of Coffee Time decorated tumblers (1964), $20-25.

Coffee Time decoration 86 oz. pitcher #86/6402 (1964), $20-25, with four #66/6402 11 ½ oz. tumblers, 5", $4-5 for each glass.

Left to right: Another version of the Fiesta Striped decoration 86 oz. pitcher, $20-30; Chestnut decoration 86 oz. pitcher, $20-30, with 11 ½ oz. tumbler, 5", $2-3 for each glass. The Fiesta Striped decoration pitcher was also produced in a version with clear vertical lines cutting through the orange stripes (Peppermint decoration #86/6611 produced in 1966). Originally this pitcher decoration was introduced on the 80 oz. pitcher made in 1938. Libbey Glass also made a similar pattern to Anchor Hocking Chestnut. Most of the glasses for the Libbey decoration are marked the capital cursive "L".

Three unidentified decorations on 86 oz. pitchers, $20-30 for each pitcher.

Three unidentified decorations on 86 oz. pitchers, $20-30 for each pitcher.

Left to right: Nordic decoration pitcher #86/6802 (1968), $20-30; two unidentified decorations on 86 oz. pitchers, $20-30 for each pitcher.

Unidentified decorations on 86 oz. pitchers, $20-30 for each pitcher.

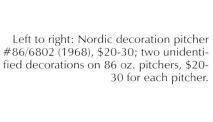

Two unidentified decorations on 86 oz. pitchers, $20-30 for each pitcher.

Three unidentified decorations on 86 oz. pitchers, $20-30 for each pitcher.

Flower Fantasy decoration on six #66/6405 11 ½ oz. tumblers (1964), 5", $2-3 for each glass. There is a matching 86 oz. pitcher with this decoration.

White Garland decoration 86 oz. pitcher #86/6814 (1968), $20-30.

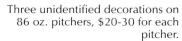
Three unidentified decorations on 86 oz. pitchers, $20-30 for each pitcher.

Four-pack of Anchor Hocking glasses with an unidentified pattern, $20-25. There is a matching 86 oz. pitcher with this decoration.

Four-pack of Classic decoration glasses (1962 to 1963), $20-25. There is a matching 86 oz. pitcher with this decoration.

Three unidentified decorations on 86 oz. pitchers, $20-30 for each pitcher.

Rare copy of the 1946 *Chain Store Age*. This publication was mainly focused on how to display and sell items (clothing, yarns, glassware, etc.) in local variety stores. Many of the items sold by Anchor Hocking were advertised in trade publications such as *Gas Station Monthly*, *Diners Digest*, *Hospital Quarterly*, or listed in the *Chain Store Age*. These publications had a very limited distribution and many are virtually impossible to find today.

Rare advertising proof that appeared in *Chain Store Age (Variety Edition)* in February 1959. Obviously, these patterns were widely distributed and reasonably easy to find today.

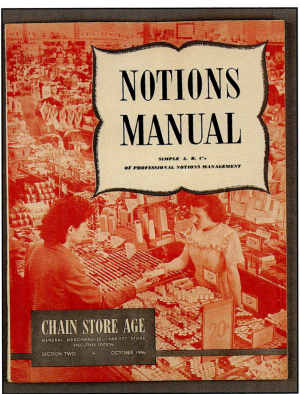

Frosted pitcher and glasses with hand-painted roses, $80-100 for the complete set with six glasses, $40-50 for the pitcher, $10-12 for each 11 oz. 4 ¾" tumbler.

Frosted pitcher and glasses with the Distlefink (Thistle Finch) decoration, $125-150 for the complete set with six glasses, $60-75 for the pitcher, $12-15 for each 11 oz. 4 ¾" tapered tumbler. The Pennsylvania Dutch (Amish) used the Distlefink on their hex signs. The Distlefink, a symbol of good luck, is perched on a heart for love and usually surrounded by tulips for faith, hope, and charity. The color blue represents truth, beauty, and spiritual strength. The yellow Distlefinks have a special significance because of their color. The color yellow represents life, sun, and gentility.

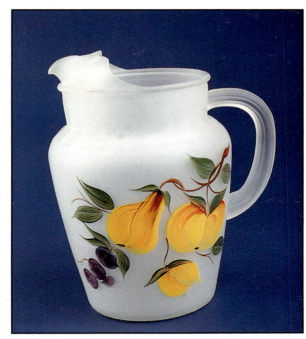

Frosted pitcher and glasses with hand-painted roses, $80-100 for the complete set with six glasses, $40-50 for the pitcher, $10-12 for each 11 oz. 4 ¾" tumbler. This set was hand-painted by the Hansetta-Artwork Studio of New York, New York.

Gay Fad Studio hand-painted this spectacular pitcher, $100-125.

Frosted pitcher and glasses, $80-100 for the complete set (with six glasses), $40-50 for the pitcher, $10-12 for each 11 oz. 4 ¾" tumbler.

Frosted pitcher and glasses with hand-painted grape vines, $80-100 for the complete set with six glasses, $40-50 for the pitcher, $10-12 for each 11 oz. 4 ¾" tumbler. I also have the matching punch bowl, oil, and vinegar bottles. Other pieces may also be available in this hand-painted pattern.

Civil War commemoratives. Left to right: vase, $30-40; 86 oz. pitcher, $40-50; 15 oz. glass, 6 ½", $10-12; 11 oz. tumbler, 4 ¾", $10-12.

The frosted pitcher commemorated the centennial of the Civil War, 1861 to 1961.

Frosted pitcher and glasses with the Ohio Indian decoration, $100-125 for the complete set (with eight glasses), $40-50 for the pitcher, $10-12 for each 15 oz. 6 ½" glass. Each glass depicts a different Native American. The names of the Native Americans are (left to right): "The Prophet, Shawnee", "Cornstalk, Shawnee", "White Eyes, Delaware", "Pontiac, Ottawa", "Tecumseh, Shawnee", "Little Turtle, Miami", "Chief Logan, Mingo", and "Blue Jacket, Shawnee" (not shown).

Frosted pitcher with the decoration for La Jolla Torrey Pines, $50-60.

Frosted pitcher with the state map of Indiana, $50-60.

The other side of the Indiana state pitcher has the state bird (cardinal).

Frosted pitcher and glasses with hand-painted flowers, $80-100 for the complete set, $40-50 for the pitcher, $10-12 for each 11 oz. 4 ¾" tumbler.

Arizona Cactus glasses given away as premiums at Blakley gas stations. The complete set consisted of eight 6 ½" glasses, $8-10 for each glass, one pitcher, $40-50, and a decorated wood rack, $50-60. Left to right: "Century Plant", "Organ Pipe", "Prickly Pear", "Yucca", 86 oz. pitcher, "Barrel", "Ocotillo", "Saguaro", and "Cholla".

Frosted pitcher with a unique design applied to the interior of the pitcher, $50-60. There is also a juice pitcher with the same pattern.

There was also a Blakley 7" cocktail/juice pitcher, $30-40, and eight 3 ¾" juice glasses (only six shown), $8-10 for each glass. This set was also available in a circular wood rack, $40-50. The glasses had the same decorations as the 6 ½" glasses.

Boxed set of Arizona Tumblers, $100-125 for the complete set, $20-30 for the box only.

There was also a crystal pitcher and glasses made in the Arizona Cactus set. The tapered glasses are marked with the Libbey capital cursive "L". I would imagine that Libbey also made the crystal pitcher.

Fired-on ribbed water bottles/juice pitchers. Left to right: Jadeite Green, $80-100; fired-on Tangerine, $80-100.

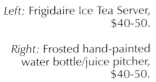

*Left:* Frigidaire Ice Tea Server, $40-50.

*Right:* Frosted hand-painted water bottle/juice pitcher, $40-50.

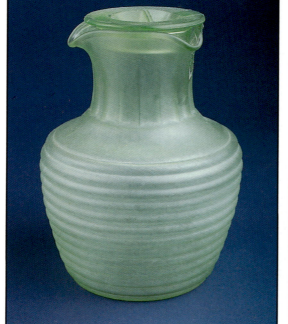

Floral water bottle/juice pitcher, $30-35, with six 10 oz. 4 ¾" tumblers, $6-8 for each tumbler.

Orchid decoration water bottle/juice pitcher, $30-35, with six 10 oz. 4 ¾" tumblers, $6-8 for each tumbler.

Floral decoration water bottle/juice pitcher, $30-35, with six 6 oz. 3 5/8" juice glasses, $6-8 for each glass.

Daisy decoration water bottle/juice pitcher, $30-35, with six 10 oz. 4 ¾" tumblers, $6-8 for each tumbler.

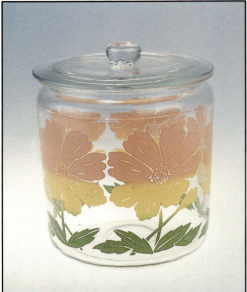

One quart provision jar and cover, $30-35.

Red Rose decoration water bottle/juice pitcher, $30-35, with four 10 oz. 4 ¾" tumblers, $6-8 for each tumbler.

Left to right: Ribbed crystal water bottle/juice pitcher with maple wood handle, $60-75; blue and white decorated water bottle/juice pitcher, $30-35; Tulip decorated water bottle/juice pitcher, $30-35. All are marked with the "anchor over H" emblem on the bottom of the bottle.

Left to right: Floral decorated water bottle/juice pitcher, $30-35; Red Rose decorated water bottle/juice pitcher, $30-35; Tomatoes and Oranges decorated water bottle/juice pitcher, $30-35. All are marked with the "anchor over H" emblem on the bottom of the bottle.

Unique plastic holder for the water bottle/juice pitcher, $60-75 for the complete set with the bottle.

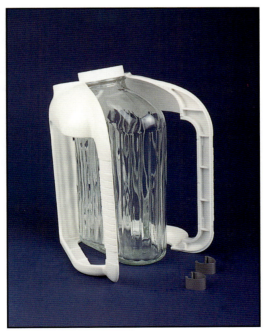

The plastic holder is hinged at the front so it can be opened to remove the water bottle. Two metal clips on the handle keep the unit together.

This Jadeite fired-on water bottle also fits the plastic holder, $80-100 for the water bottle.

Wrought Iron decoration on the 40 oz. juice pitcher, $20-30, with six 6 oz. 3 7/8" juice glasses, $3-4 for each glass. The glasses have the Dominion Glass capital cursive "D" on the bottom of each glass.

Left to right: Oranges and Tomatoes decoration 40 oz. juice pitcher (1960), $20-25; Crystal 40 oz. juice pitcher, $20-30; Tomatoes decoration 40 oz. juice pitcher #246/814 (1959), $20-25.

Futuristic decoration on the 40 oz. juice pitcher, $20-30, with eight 6 oz. 3 ½" juice glasses, $3-4 for each glass

Tomatoes decoration 7-Piece Juice Set #400/120, $50-60 for the complete set, $5-10 for the box only.

Fiesta Bands decoration 40 oz. chiller with red plastic top (1959), $20-25, with four 6 oz. 3 ½" juice glasses, $1-2 for each glass.

Left to right: Oranges decoration 40 oz. chiller #3340/813 (1961), $15-20; Coral Tulip decoration 40 oz. chiller, $20-25.

Oranges decoration 7-Piece Juice Set #3300/180 (1964), $30-40 for the complete set, $5-10 for the box only.

Oranges decoration 7-Piece Juice Set #3300/146, (1959), $30-40 for the complete set, $5-10 for the box only.

71

Oranges decoration 40 oz. chiller #283/367 (1957 to 1958), $15-20, with six 6 oz. 3 ¾" juice glasses, $1-2 for each glass.

Bimbo Child's Tumbler Set #3300/232 (1966), $75-80 for the complete set, $15-20 for the box only.

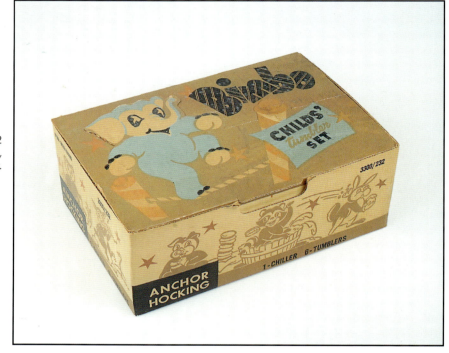

The Bimbo Child's Tumbler Set includes one 40 oz chiller, $20-25, and six 6 oz. 4 ¾" juice glasses, $4-5 for each glass. The juice glasses are decorated and named for the figure on each glass. Left to right (glasses only): "Cubby", "Bimbo", "Piggy", "Bunny", "Coony", and "Lambsy". All seven pieces are labeled with the "anchor over H" emblem.

Assorted 54 oz. chillers, $10-15 for each decoration.

Assorted 50 oz. chillers, $10-15 for each decoration.

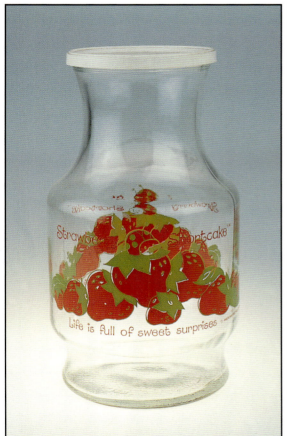

Strawberry Shortcake decoration 54 oz. chiller, $20-25.

Assorted 54 oz. chillers, $10-15 for each decoration.

Super Fruit 5-Piece Juice Set #3600/636 (1974), $25-30 for the complete set, $10-15 for the 54 oz. Super Plum chiller with cap, $1-2 for each Super Apple, Super Pear, Super Lemon, and Super Orange glass.

73

One dozen Super Lemon 7 oz. juice glasses, $30-35, $5-10 for the box only.

One dozen Super Orange 7 oz. juice glasses, $30-35, $5-10 for the box only.

Rooster Morn 5-Piece Juice Set, $25-30 for the complete set, $4-5 for the box only.

Four-pack of Super Fruit 7 oz. juice glasses, $10-15 for the complete set.

Tulip decoration 54 oz. chiller, $10-15, with four 6 oz. 3 ½" juice glasses, $1-2 for each glass.

Goose decoration 54 oz. chiller, $10-15, with six 15 oz. 6 ¼" iced teas, $1-2 for each glass, and one 26 oz. 5 ¼" jar, $3-5.

Apple decoration 54 oz. chiller, $10-15.

Four-pack of Oranges decoration juice glasses, $10-15 for the complete set.

Four-pack of Oranges decoration juice glasses, $10-15 for the complete set.

# CHAPTER EIGHT

# Frosted Juice Pitchers

Hand-painted 40 oz. juice pitcher, $30-40, with six 5 oz. juice glasses, 3 5/8", $4-5 for each glass.

Hand-painted 40 oz. juice pitcher, $30-40, with six 4 oz. juice glasses, 2 7/8", $4-5 for each glass.

Hand-painted 40 oz. juice pitcher, $30-40, with six 5 oz. juice glasses, 3 ¾", $4-5 for each glass.

Hand-painted 40 oz. juice pitcher, $30-40, with six 5 oz. juice glasses, 3 ¾", $4-5 for each glass.

Hand-painted 40 oz. juice pitcher, $30-40, with six 4 oz. juice glasses, 2 7/8", $4-5 for each glass.

Left to right: 40 oz. juice pitcher decorated and marked by Gay Fad Studio, $40-50; 40 oz. juice pitcher marked with "Lake to Lake, we own it, it's our own business", $40-45.

Hand-painted 40 oz. juice pitcher, $30-40.

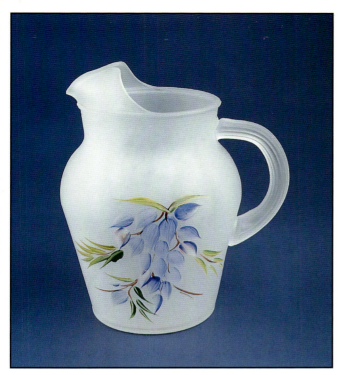

*Center:* 100th anniversary set from the State of Oregon. This set was issued in 1959. The set includes one frosted juice pitcher, $30-40, with eight 15 oz. tumblers, 5 1/8", $10-12 for each glass, and one pine wood tray, $50-60.

*Bottom:* Left to right: "Bonneville Dam"; "Oregon's 100th Anniversary"; "Three Sisters"; "Silver Creek"; 40 oz. juice with "State of Oregon"; "Metolins River"; "Crater Lake"; "Mount Hood"; "Coast Line".

Set of 1964 World's Fair glasses, $100-125, $20-30 for the box only.

Historic glasses distributed by the Frontier Refining Company, 4040 East Louisiana Avenue, Denver 22, Colorado, $80-100 for the entire set, $20-30 for the cardboard holder only.

The historic set consisted of eight glasses. Left to right: "Showdown"; "Roundup"; "Iron Horse"; "Cliff Dwellers"; "Rush for Gold"; "Black Gold"; "Gold Strike" (not shown) and "Frontier Society" (not shown).

Left to right: "The Unisphere"; "World's Fair Circus"; "William A. Shea Stadium"; "The Federal Pavilion"; "New York State Exhibit"; "Pool of Industry"; "Port Authority Building"; and "Hall of Science". The glasses are all marked with the familiar "anchor over H" emblem on the bottom of the glass.

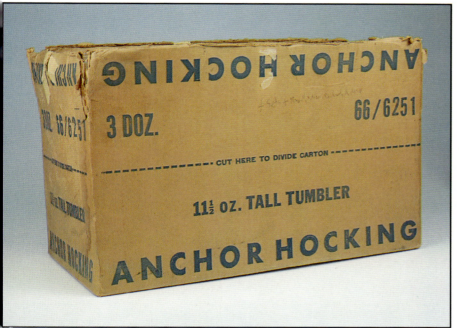

Boxed set of 11 ½ oz. tumblers, $80-100 for the set, $10-15 for the box only.

Left to right: "1900 Oldsmobile"; "1902 Packard"; "1906 Stanley Steamer"; "1906 Autocar"; "1908 Buick"; "1909 Nash Rambler"; "1911 Maxwell"; and "1913 Hudson".

The automobile glasses were made in two sizes. Left to right: 15 oz. tumbler, 6 ½", $3-4; 11 ½ oz. tumbler, 5", $5-8. The smaller size tumblers are harder to find and both sizes of tumblers are marked with the "anchor over H" emblem in the bottom of the glass.

Frosted 10 oz. pilsners, 7 ½", $8-10 for each glass. There are other frosted pilsners with Papa, Mama, and Uncle Bertie. Since most sets were sold in groups of four or eight, I would guess that there probably are three more different deco-rated frosted glasses that exist.

The 15 oz. tumblers. Left to right: "1900 Oldsmobile"; "1902 Packard"; "1906 Stanley Steamer"; "1906 Autocar"; "1908 Buick"; "1909 Nash Rambler"; "1911 Max-well"; and "1913 Hudson".

California mission set of glasses, $60-80 for a set of marked glasses. Left to right: "Mission San Francisco de Asis"; "Mission Santa Barbara"; "Mission San Jose de Guadalupe"; "Mission San Gabriel Arcangel"; "Mission San Juan Bautista"; "Mission San Carlos Borromeo de Carmelo"; "Mission San Juan Capristrano"; and "Mission Santa Clara de Asis". All the glasses produced and sold were not marked; however, each decoration can be found with the "anchor over H" emblem.

Frosted 10 oz. pilsners with 22 kt. gold lines, 7 ½",
$10-12 for each glass.

The Gay Nineties set of glasses were made in clear and frosted versions. This set includes the "Bicycle for Two", "The Hansom", "Gas Buggy", and "Horse Car" (not shown), $5-8 for each glass. The clear versions were made in at least three different color variations.

Hand-painted 12 oz. glasses marked with the "anchor over H" emblem in the bottom of the glass, 5 ¼", $10-15 for each glass.

Red Squares 15 oz. tumblers #3526/5650 (1957 to 1958), 6 ½", $3-5 for each tumbler. This decoration was also made with squares in black, red, and blue.

Polka Dot frosted 15 oz. glasses, 6 ½", $10-15 for each glass.

Frosted Newport design 12 oz. glasses, 5", $2-3 for each glass.

Set of 15 oz. 6 ½" glasses with scenes of California, $5-8 for each glass. There are probably eight glasses in the entire set. Left to right: "Joshua Trees"; "Lake Arrowhead"; "Santa Monica"; "Santa Catalina"; and "Mission San Juan De Capistrano". These glasses were given away at gas stations along with the La Jolla Torrey Pines pitcher shown earlier in this text.

Left to right: Ohio 15 oz. glass, 6 ½", $5-8; Professional Football Hall of Fame 15 oz. glass, 6 ½", $5-10.

Frosted with Gold and Red Bands decoration (1938 to 1942). Left to right: 80 oz. pitcher, $40-50; 42 oz. pitcher, $30-40.

Frosted with Gold and Red Bands decoration 80 oz. pitcher, $40-50, with two goblets, 7", $15-20 for each goblet.

Frosted with Gold and Red Bands decoration 80 oz. pitcher, $40-50, with six goblets, 7", $20-25 for each goblet.

Frosted with Gold and Red Bands decoration 80 oz. pitcher, $40-50, with three #182/2585 3 ½ oz. blown cocktails on the left, 3", $10-15 each, and three #3505/2585 12 oz. blown highballs, 5 ½", $10-15 each, on the right.

Frosted with Gold and Red Bands decoration 80 oz. pitcher, $40-50, with four goblets, 7", $20-25 for each goblet.

Left to right: 32 oz. cocktail shaker #749/2585, 10", $30-40; 7 ½ oz. pressed old fashioned, 3", $15-20; 1 ½ oz. #64/2585 blown whiskey, 1 ½", $10-15.

Left to right: Orange decoration 42 oz. juice pitcher #746/4594 (1938 to 1942), $20-25; 42 oz. juice pitcher #746/34 (1948), $20-25.

Two color versions of the 42 oz. juice pitcher with orchid decorations, $25-30 for each color version.

Two hand-painted versions of the 42 oz. pitcher, $30-40 for each version.

Frosted 80 oz. tilt ball pitcher with platinum lines, $40-50, with four 12 oz. glasses, 4 ¾", $10-12 for each glass.

Frosted 80 oz. tilt ball pitcher with platinum lines, $40-50, with four 3 ½ oz. cocktails, 3", $10-12 for each glass.

Swirl tilt ball pitchers. Left to right: crystal version, $20-30; rare pink version, $100-125.

Target Line 80 oz. pitcher, $40-50, with four 15 oz. glasses, 5 ½", $10-15 for each glass.

Hobnail 80 oz. pitcher, $40-50, with four 15 oz. glasses, 5 ½", $10-15 for each glass.

Left to right: 15 oz. glass, 5 ½", $10-15; 12 oz. glass, 4 ¾", $10-12; 6 oz. juice, 4", $8-10.

Waffle 80 oz. pitcher, $40-50, with six 12 oz. glasses, 4 ¾", $10-15 for each glass.

Hand-painted 42 oz. juice pitcher, $30-40, with six 3 ½ oz. cocktails, 2 ½", $5-8 for each glass.

Hand-painted 42 oz. juice pitcher, $30-40, with one 3 ½ oz. cocktail, 2 ½", $5-8.

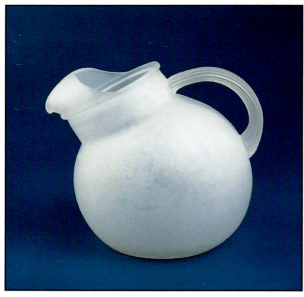

Plain frosted 80 oz. pitcher, $30-40.

Hand-painted 42 oz. juice pitcher, $30-40, with four Roly Poly 5 oz. juice glasses, 2 ½", $5-8 for each glass.

Left to right: Fired-on pink 80 oz. pitcher, $60-75; 42 oz. fired-on pink juice pitcher, $50-60.

Fired-on green 80 oz. pitcher, $60-75, with six flared tumblers, 4 ½", $10-15 for each glass. Notice the difference in the color in the last two tumblers on the right. The same color variations occur in the other colors of the fired-on glasses.

Fired-on blue glassware. Left to right: 10 oz. glass, 4 ½", $10-15; 80 oz. pitcher, $60-75; 6 oz. juice glass, 4", $12-15; 42 oz. juice pitcher, $50-60.

Fired-on tangerine glassware. Left to right: 10 oz. glass, 4 ½", $10-15; 80 oz. Ball Jug #787/2157 (1938 to 1942), $60-75; 6 oz. juice glass, 4", $12-15; 42 oz. Ball Jug #746/2157 (1938 to 1942), $50-60.

Fired-on yellow glassware. Left to right: 10 oz. glass in light yellow, 4 ½", $12-15; 10 oz. glass in dark yellow, 4 ½", $10-15; 80 oz. pitcher, $60-75; 6 oz. juice glass, 4", $12-15; 42 oz. juice pitcher, $50-60.

Two different colors of the 15 oz. iced tea, 6", $15-20 for each color.

### Park Avenue

[A] 86240 Park Avenue Small Bowl 6" Open Stock
[B] 86242 Park Avenue Luncheon Plate 8" Open Stock
[C] 86243 Park Avenue Dinner Plate 10" Open Stock
[D] 69886 Park Avenue 10 oz. Rocks Open Stock
[E] 69887 Park Avenue 16 oz. Cooler Open Stock

### Victoria

[F] 87525 2 pc. 13.5" Footed Cake/Dome Gift Boxed
[G] 87527 2 pc. 13.5" Chip Plate & Dip Bowl Gift Boxed
[H] 87533 4 pc. Footed Dessert Bowl Set Gift Boxed
[I] 87526 1 pc. Footed Trifle Gift Boxed
[J] 87779 5 pc Salad Set Gift Boxed
(1 - Large Bowl, 4 - Small Bowls)

### Melon

[K] 83466 17 oz. Tumbler Open Stock
[L] 83265 64 oz. Pitcher Open Stock

### Ribbed

[M] 83468 9 oz. Juice Open Stock
[N] 83467 64 oz. Chiller w/Glass Lid Open Stock

### Union Square

[O] 86436 Bowl 4.75" Open Stock
[P] 86437 Bowl 6" Open Stock
[Q] 86438 Bowl 8.5" Open Stock
[R] 86439 Plate 9" Open Stock
[S] 86441 Platter 12" Open Stock

Anchor Hocking began to re-introduce many older patterns under new names. You will notice that the crystal tilt ball pitcher has been re-introduced into the market under the name Melon. The design has not been changed and even the rings on the neck are horizontal like the original. Unlike the earlier version, Anchor Hocking did produce a glass to go with the pitcher. You will also notice that the ribbed water bottle has also been re-introduced with a glass and plastic lid. Ribs were added to the neck to distinguish the modern version from the older versions. Even the original Charm pattern was re-introduced in Crystal and called Union Square.

Left to right: crystal 80 oz. pitcher (still being made by Anchor Hocking), $15-20; fired-on Tangerine 80 oz. pitcher, $50-75.

Three versions of the Manhattan 42 oz. pitcher. Left to right: pink fired-on pitcher, $30-40; crystal pitcher, $20-25; tangerine fired-on pitcher, $25-30.

The 80 oz. pitcher with etched deer, $50-75, with two 12 oz. glasses, 4 ¾", $10-15 for each glass.

The 80 oz. pitcher with etched flying geese, $50-75, with four 12 oz. glasses, 4 ¾", $10-15 for each glass.

The 80 oz. pitcher with etched floral decorations, $50-75, with four 12 oz. glasses, 4 ¾", $10-15 for each glass.

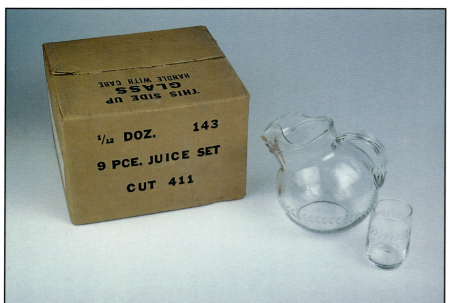

Nine-piece juice set with Cut #401 etching, $60-75 for the complete set, $10-15 for the box only.

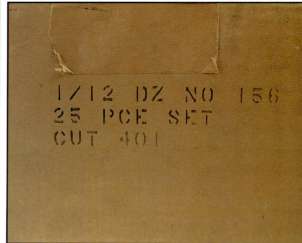

Twenty five-piece set of Cut #401, $125-150 for the complete set, $15-20 for the box only.

Opened box so you can see the arrangement of the glassware. The smallest glasses are on either side of the pitcher and the 9 oz. table tumblers are directly under the larger 15 oz. iced teas on the top.

The 25-piece set included one 80 oz pitcher, $30-40, eight 5 oz. #3363 juice glasses, 3 ¾", $3-5, eight 9 oz. #3361 table tumblers, 4 ½", $3-5, and eight 15 oz. iced tea glasses #3369, 5 ¼", $3-5.

Silver Laurel etching. Left to right: 80 oz. pitcher, $30-40; 42 oz. pitcher, $25-30.

*Bottom four photos:* Etched 80 oz. pitchers, $30-40.

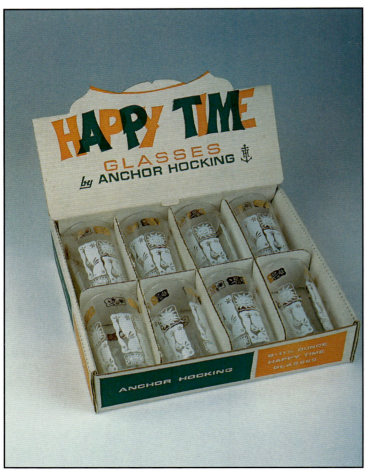

Set #66-2/3-C-33 with stylized birds and gold designs on 5" straight shell glasses, $20-30 for the set of eight glasses with the box.

Set #3172-2/3-SF1 with two tone green and gold designs on 5 ½" heavy based glasses, $30-40 for the set of eight glasses with the box.

*Opposite page;*
*Top left:* Set #65-2/3-C5 with white flowers and gold designs on 4 ¾" straight shell glasses, $20-30 for the set of eight glasses with the box.

*Top right:* Set #3616-2/3-C10 with stylized flowers in blue, yellow, brown, and pink on 5 ½" heavy based glasses, $20-30 for the set of eight glasses with the box.

*Bottom left:* Song Bird Set (1974) #3582-2/3-FA10 with pictures of the Baltimore oriole, chickadee, blue jay, and cardinal designs on 4 ¾" Finlandia glasses, $30-40 for the set of eight glasses with the box.

*Bottom right:* Set #3526-2/3-39 with colonial lady designs on 6 ½" frosted glasses in crystal, pink, yellow, and light green, $25-35 for the set of eight glasses with the box.

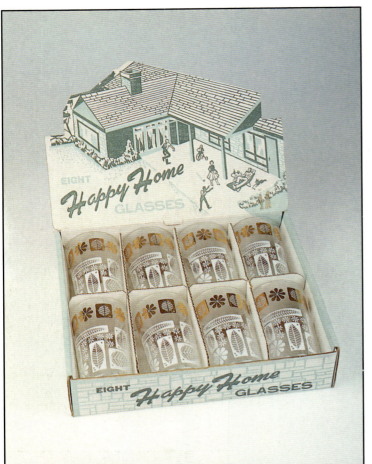

*Top:* Set #65-2/3-C17 with stylized leaves and gold designs on 4 ¾" straight shell glasses, $20-30 for the set of eight glasses with the box.
*Bottom:* Set #400/79-BANDS with red, white, green, yellow, and orange stripes on 5 1/8" tapered glasses, $25-30 for the set of eight glasses with the box.

*Top:* Set #65-2/3-C5 with red, white, green, yellow, and orange stripes on 4 ¾" straight shell glasses, $20-30 for the set of eight glasses with the box.
*Bottom:* Set #3616-2/3-C15 with aqua and gold designs on 5 ½" heavy based glasses, $20-35 for the set of eight glasses with the box.

Set #65-2/3-C18 with ballerinas and gold designs on 4 ¾" straight shell glasses, $25-30 for the set of eight glasses with the box.

Set #479-2/3-38 with white diamonds and gold lines on 4 ¾" straight shell glasses, $40-50 for the set of eight glasses with the box.

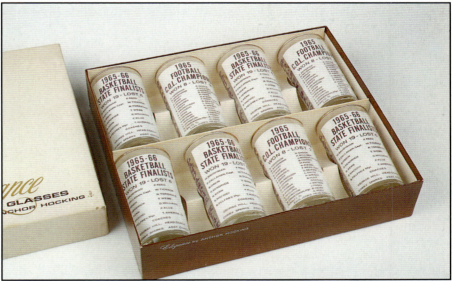

The diamond and gold line glasses were available in two sizes, the 4 ¾" glass on the left and the 3 ¼" glass on the right, $4-5 for each glass. I have seen these glasses sold with another pitcher definitely not made by Anchor Hocking.

Set of 5 ½" heavy based glasses with the members of the 1965 Football and 1965-1966 Basketball champions from Lancaster High School, $20-30 for the set of eight glasses with the box.

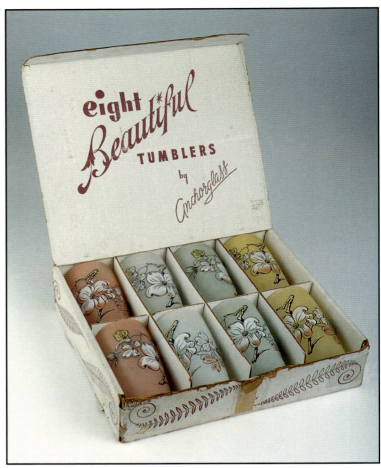

*Top:* Set of 5 1/8" heaved based glasses with Oriental lady and gold leaf designs, $25-35 for the set of eight glasses with the box.

*Bottom:* Set #3616-2/3-F7 with four different designs on 5 ½" heavy based glasses, $25-30 for the set of eight glasses with the box. The designs are "Horse Car", "Gas Buggy", "The Hansom", and "Bicycle for Two". This particular set was issued many times in different boxes. Each time it was issued, the colors on the pictures were changed.

Set of 5 5/8" tapered frosted glasses with dogwood designs in red, yellow, light green, and crystal, $25-30 for the set of eight glasses with the box.

Another set of the "Horse Car", "Gas Buggy", "The Hansom", and "Bicycle for Two", $25-30 for the set of eight glasses with the box.

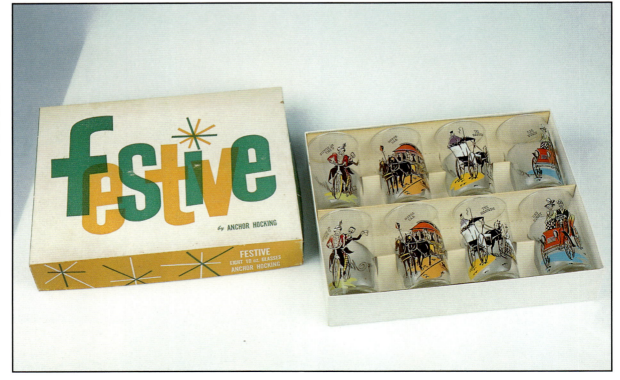

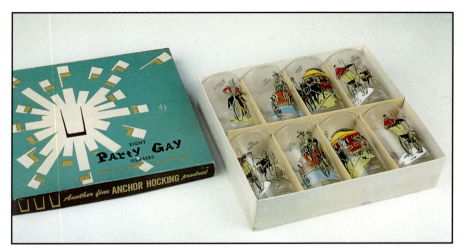

Another set of the "Horse Car", "Gas Buggy", "The Hansom", and "Bicycle for Two", $25-30 for the set of eight glasses with the box.

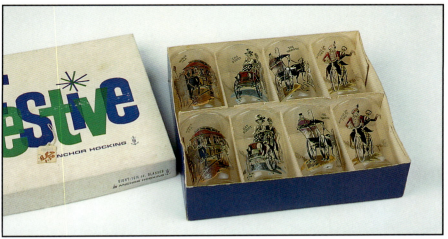

Set #3614-2/3-F25 with four different designs on 5 ½" heavy based glasses, $25-30 for the set of eight glasses with the box. The designs in this set have a metallic finish. American Hardware Stores sold this set for only $1.50.

Set #66-2/3-F31 with pictures of kitchen items on 5" straight shell glasses, $25-30 for the set of eight glasses with the box.

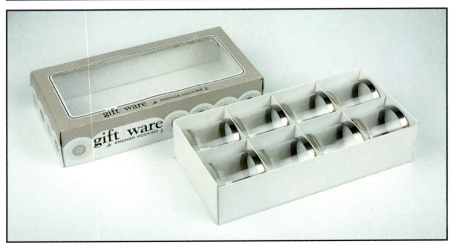

Set with platinum rims on eight 3" heavy based glasses, $25-30 for the set of eight glasses with the box.

Set #66-2/3-F39 with musical instruments and notes on 5" straight shell glasses, $25-30 for the set of eight glasses with the box.

Set with floral designs on 5 ¼" glasses, $25-30 for the set of eight glasses with the box.

Set #415-2/3-8 with orange and white stripes on 4 ¾" straight shell glasses, $25-30 for the set of eight glasses with the box.

Set with aqua and gold floral designs on 5 ½" heavy based glasses, $30-35 for the set of eight glasses with the box.

Set #3624-2/3-F10 with floral decorations on 5" Newport design glasses, $25-30 for the set of eight glasses with the box.

Set with heart decorations on 5" Newport design glasses, $25-30 for the set of eight glasses with the box.

Set with floral decorations on 3" Finlandia design glasses, $25-30 for the set of eight glasses with the box.

Boxed set #3500/451-2/3-C2 contains eight Finlandia design 9 oz. 3" on-the-rocks, $20-25 for the complete set, $5-8 for the box only. There are two each of the following glasses in the set: "The Cocked Hat Tavern", "1783 Black Horse Tavern", "1808 Temperance", and "1761 Silent Woman Entertainment".

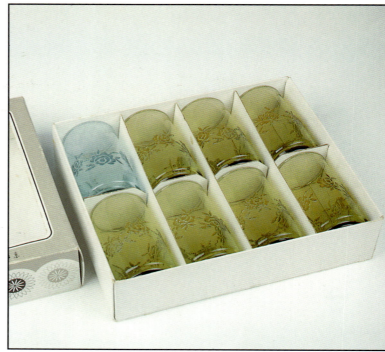

Boxed set #3500/384-1/3-S2 contained four 2 ½" shot glasses, $15-20 for the complete set, $3-5 for the box only. There are one of each of the following glasses in the set: "The Cocked Hat Tavern", "1783 Black Horse Tavern", "1808 Temperance", and "1761 Silent Woman Entertainment".

Boxed set of eight Finlandia design 12 oz. 4 ¾" beverage glasses, $25-30 for the complete set, $5-8 for the box only. I included one beverage glass in Aquamarine to show that the set was made in more than one color.

Boxed set #3654-2/3-SFC1 contained eight 8 oz. 3" on-the-rocks, $30-40 for the complete set, $5-10 for the box only.

Boxed set #3614-2/3-C31 contained eight 12 oz. 5" heavy based glasses, $25-30 for the complete set, $5-10 for the box only.

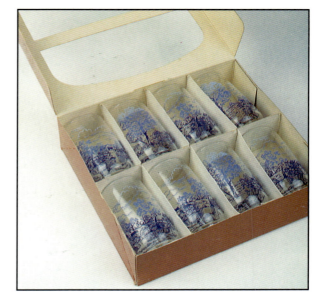

"Heydays, as We Were" boxed set of eight 5 ½" heavy based glasses, $40-50 for the complete set, $10-15 for the box only. The set contained two each of the following images: a lady dangling her feet in the water as she sits on a dock, a bicycle rider, woman putting on the golf course, and a couple in an antique automobile.

*Top right:* Boxed set #3624-2/3-F7 contained eight 12 ½ oz. 5" Newport design glasses, $25-30 for the complete set, $5-10 for the box only.

Boxed set #9616-2/3-FA3 contained eight 15 oz. 5 ½" heavy base iced teas, $35-50 for the complete set, $5-10 for the box only. The set includes two each of the following glasses: violet, daisy, tulip and rose.

Boxed set #3672-2/3-F7 contained eight 12 ½ oz. 5 ¼" beverage glasses, $25-30 for the complete set, $5-10 for the box only.

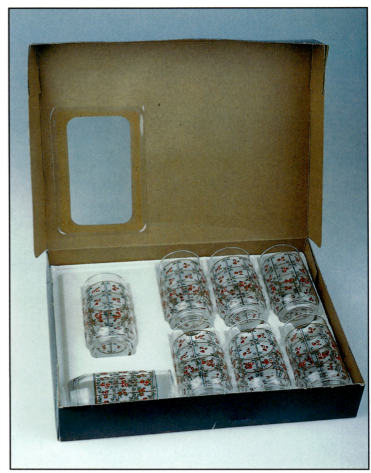

Boxed set #3172-2/3-FA19 contained eight 12 oz. 5 ½" Chateau design glasses, $25-30 for the complete set, $5-10 for the box only.

Boxed set containing eight 12 ½ oz. 5" Newport design glasses, $25-30 for the complete set, $5-10 for the box only.

Royal Crest boxed set #8600/20 contained eight 12 oz. 5 ½" heavy base glasses, $40-50 for the complete set, $5-10 for the box only. This set is very ornate with 22 kt. gold design decorations.

Boxed set #3539V/4790 contained six 12 oz. 5" tapered glasses, $30-40 for the complete set, $5-10 for the box only. Each glass is decorated with "Evan Williams since 1783, Kentucky's 1st Distiller. No whiskey on earth can satisfy you more."

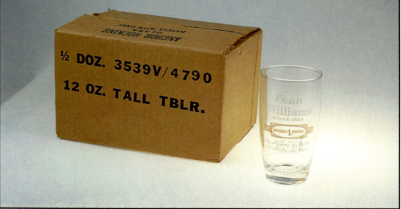

Boxed set #3537H/1919 contained six 3 ½" tapered glasses, $30-40 for the complete set, $5-10 for the box only. Each glass is decorated with "Heaven Hill, the <u>BEST</u> of the Great Kentucky Bourbons."

Boxed set #65K/6233 contained twelve Chantilly decoration 11 ½ oz. 4 ¾" glasses with 22 kt. gold rims, $25-30 for the complete set, $5-10 for the box only.

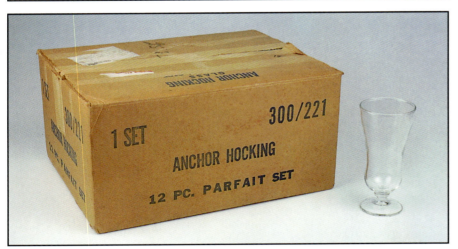

Boxed set #300/221 contained twelve 5 7/8" parfait glasses, $25-30 for the complete set, $5-10 for the box only.

Boxed set #66-2/3-F30 contained eight 11 oz. 4 ¾" glasses with 22 kt. gold rims, $25-30 for the complete set, $5-10 for the box only. All the glasses are marked with the "anchor over H" emblem.

Boxed set #2501 contained thirty-six Savoy 1 oz. 4" cordials, $25-30 for the complete set, $5-10 for the box only.

Boxed set #3113L/945 Holiday Magic contained twelve 12 oz. 4" heavy base double on-the-rocks, $20-25 for the complete set, $5-10 for the box only.

Boxed set #3600/597 Gold Coin contained eight 10 ½ oz. 5" heavy base glasses, $30-40 for the complete set, $5-10 for the box only. Each glass depicts seven different antique coins from countries around the globe.

Boxed set #3600/424 contained eight 10 ½ oz. 5" heavy base glasses, $25-30 for the complete set, $5-10 for the box only. The tumblers state, "Being an occasion to celebrate 100 grand years of service to the petroleum industry. Oil Well Supply centennial, 1862 to 1962."

Boxed set #3513K/4343 contained twelve Canadian Club Whiskey 10 oz. 4 ¼" glasses with 22 kt. gold rims, $30-40 for the complete set, $5-10 for the box only.

Twenty-four piece beverage set contained twelve 18 oz. 5 ¾" iced teas and twelve 12 ½ oz. 3 ¾" on-the-rocks, $30-35 for the complete set, $5-10 for the box only.

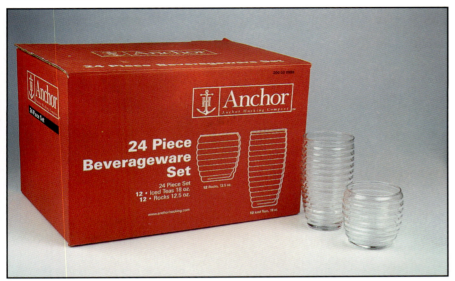

Boxed set #3100/132-1/12-C4 contained twelve zodiac 13 oz. 4" heavy base glasses with 22 kt. gold zodiac designs, $40-50 for the complete set, $10-15 for the box only.

The Zodiac glasses were also made in a large 12 oz. 5 ½" heavy based glass, $3-5 for each glass.

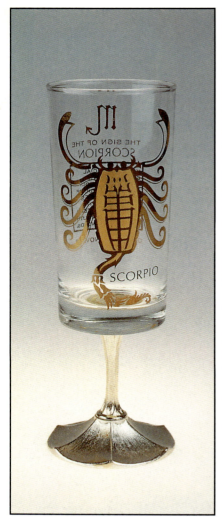

Zodiac glass fastened to a metal stem to make a candle, 8 ½" to the top of the glass, $10-15.

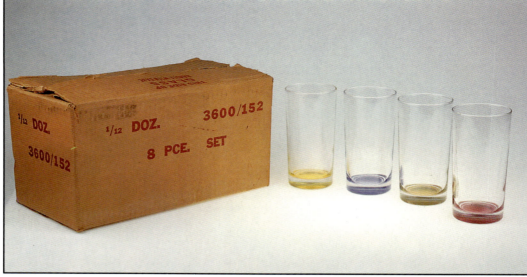

*Top:* Yellow Rose boxed set #100/101 contained eight 11 ½ oz. 5" heavy base glasses with 22 kt. gold rims, $25-30 for the complete set, $5-10 for the box only.

*Bottom:* Boxed set #3600/152 contained eight 15 oz. 5 5/8" heavy base glasses with colored bases, $30-40 for the complete set, $5-10 for the box only. The set includes two glasses with each having either a blue, green, yellow or red base.

Heritage Holly boxed set #1023-96 contained twelve 16 oz. 6" Newport design glasses, $25-30 for the complete set, $5-10 for the box only.

Boxed set #3000/100 of four Oldsmobile Vintage Car 5 ½" glasses, $30-40 for the complete set, $5-10 for the box only. The glasses have the following designs: "The First Automobile 1897", "Curved Dash Oldsmobile 1903", "Oldsmobile Limited 1910", and "Oldsmobile Convertible Coupe 1928." The box also states, "Oldsmobile, for 75 years always a step ahead."

Georges Briard set of four 14 oz. 4 1/8" heavy base glasses, $20-25 for the complete set, $5-10 for the box only. The Georges Briard signature is visible on each glass.

Twelve Days of Christmas boxed set #3600/769 contained twelve 12 oz. 5" Newport design glasses, $25-30 for the complete set, $5-10 for the box only. Each glass has a design for the specific day in the song "The Twelve Days of Christmas."

Twelve Days of Christmas boxed set #3100/328 contained twelve 12 ½ oz. 5 ½" heavy base tumblers, $25-30 for the complete set, $5-10 for the box only. Each glass has a design for the specific day in the song "The Twelve Days of Christmas."

Cut crystal boxed set #J3600/666 contained six 13 oz. 5" Roly Poly design coolers, six 9 oz. 4 ¼" Roly Poly design beverage glasses and six 9 oz. 2 ¾" Roly Poly design on-the-rocks glasses, $50-60 for the complete set, $5-10 for the box only.

Ten piece beverage set that was made by Anchor Glass Container. Anchor Hocking Glass Corporation did not make this set. There is some confusion between the two companies and the company names. Be careful when purchasing this glassware!!!

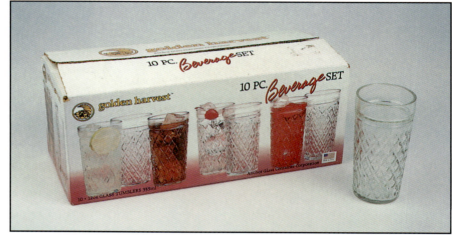

Country Accents set #2900/89 consists of four 6 ½ oz. 6 ¼" wine glasses, $15-20 for the complete set, $3-5 for the box only.

Country Accents set #3100/303 consists of four 12 ½ oz. 5 ½" heavy base glasses, $15-20 for the complete set, $3-5 for the box only.

Set of four 3 3/8" heavy base on-the-rocks, $20-30 for the complete set, $5-10 for the box only. Each glass has Anchor Hocking with the company emblem on one side and the other side states "Bouncing Back, the Commitment Continues." All the glasses are rimmed in 22 kt. gold.

Unique set of 5 ½ oz. #2405/6767 champagne glasses with multicolored iridescent coatings, $40-50 for the complete set, $5-10 for the box only. These 4 ½" glasses are part of the Nocturne Stemware listed in the 1968 catalog. This iridescent decoration was applied to three Baltic design glasses, the Baltic sherbet, the Accent Modern chip and dip set, four different apothecary jars, and five different stemware glasses.

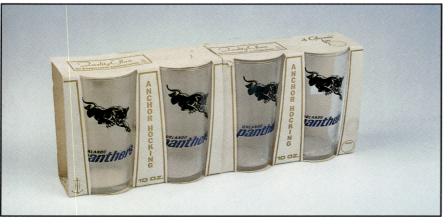

Four-pack of Orlando Panthers 10 oz. beverage glasses, $15-20 for the complete set.

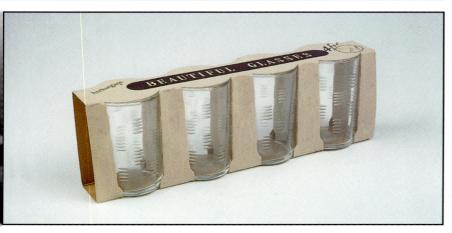

Four-pack of Cascade Cutting (Cut #404) 10 oz. 3 ½" beverage glasses, $15-20 for the complete set.

Four-pack of Balmoral Harness Racing Inc. 10 oz. 4 7/8" beverage glasses, $15-20 for the complete set.

Four-pack of Berwick 4 oz. juice/wine 4 ½" glasses, $15-20 for the complete set.

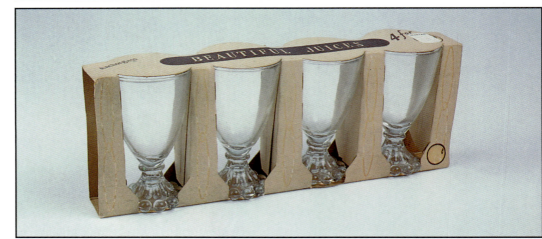

Four-pack of Splash O' Color decorated 6 oz. 3 ¾" juice glasses, $15-20 for the complete set. There is an 86 oz. pitcher with this decoration (1969).

Two 4-packs of Roly Poly Laurel Cutting 9 oz. 4 3/8" glasses, $15-20 for the each complete set.

114

Carrier with four 11 oz. 4 ¾" glasses with an unidentified pattern, $20-30.

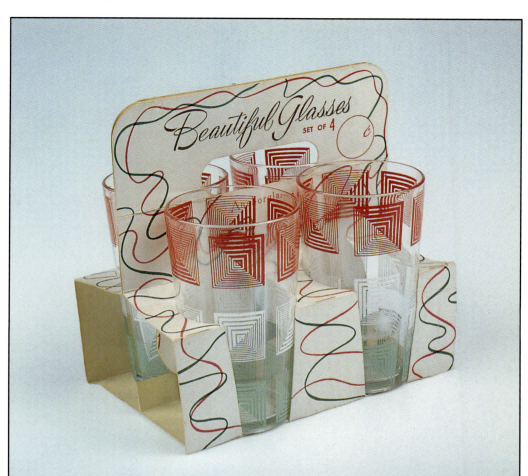

Carrier with four 11 oz. 4 ¾" glasses with an unidentified pattern, $20-30.

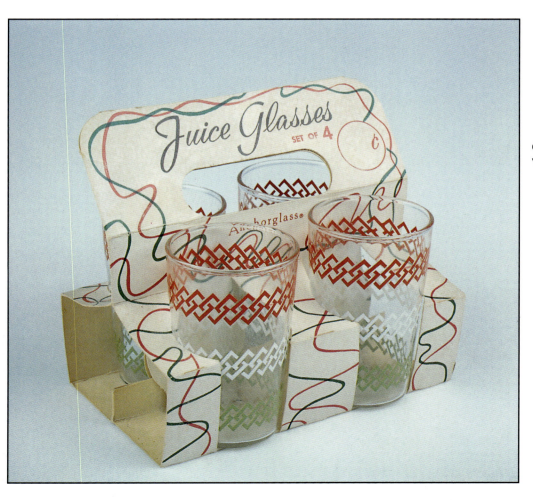

Etched cocktail shaker with chrome plated lid, 9 ½" to the top of the lid, $30-40.

Cocktail shaker with plastic lid, 9" to the top of the lid, $20-30. The shaker is marked with the "anchor over H" on the bottom.

Irvinware stainless steel cocktail shaker, 8 ¼" to the top of the shaker, with four 3" on-the-rocks with colored bases, $40-50 for the complete set, $10-15 for the shaker and $4-5 for each glass. The glasses have four different colored bases and each is marked with the "anchor over H" emblem.

Cocktail set with carrier. The set includes one 7 ¼" shaker, $20-30, eight Baltic 3 ½ oz. 2 ¾" cocktails with gold band and hairline decoration in 22 kt. gold, $2-3 for each glass, and one brass coated holder, $5-10. The shaker is plastic coated with a glass insert. The insert is marked with the "anchor over H" emblem.

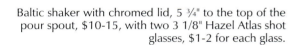

Baltic shaker with chromed lid, 5 ¾" to the top of the pour spout, $10-15, with two 3 1/8" Hazel Atlas shot glasses, $1-2 for each glass.

Baltic shaker with chromed lid and a diamond cut "Ours", 5 ¾" to the top of the pour spout, $10-15, with two 3" shot glasses, $1-2 for each glass.

Left to right: Anchor Hocking 3 ½ oz. cocktail, 3", $2-3 depending on the decoration; Libbey 3 oz. cocktail, 3", $1-2 depending on the decoration. Notice the Libbey cocktail is the same height but smaller in diameter. Most of the Libbey cocktails are marked with the capital cursive "L".

*Center right:* The Outdoorsman 6-Piece Cocktail Set contained four Finlandia design 3" glasses, one Finlandia design 7" cocktail shaker, and one brass plated mixing spoon, $20-30 for the complete set, $5-10 for the box only. Each glass has either the wild turkey, bobwhite quail, black duck or ring-necked pheasant decoration. The cocktail shaker has all four bird decorations.

The Finlandia 6-Piece Cocktail Set contained four Finlandia design 3" glasses with platinum decorations, one Finlandia design 7" cocktail shaker with platinum decorations, and one chrome plated mixing spoon, $40-50 for the complete set, $5-10 for the box only. The set included a hostess book listing stemware and tumbler service guide with several non-alcoholic beverage recipes, $10-15 for the hostess book only.

The 7-Piece Crystal Ball Beverage Set contained one cocktail shaker and six 4 ½ oz. 2 ¾" Beverly cocktail glasses, $60-75 for the complete set, $15-20 for the box only. The Armour Grocery Products Company of Chicago, Illinois, distributed the set.

The Happy Hour 8-Piece Cocktail Sets in both red and green colors, $30-40 for each set, $10-15 for the box only.

Cocktail sets were also made with one 7 ½" giant mixer, $10-15, and six 3 ½ oz. 3" footed cocktail glasses, $1-2 for each glass.

Each Happy Hour 8-Piece Cocktail Set included one 32 oz. 6 ¼" mixer, six 4 ½ oz. 2 ¾" Beverly cocktail glasses and one brass plated mixing spoon.

The 8-Piece Cocktail Set #3200/101-1, $30-40, contained one 32 oz. 6 ¼" mixer, six 4 oz. 2 ½" Beverly cocktail glasses, and one brass plated spoon.

The 8-Piece Cocktail Set #3200/103, $30-40, contained one 32 oz. 6 ¼" mixer, six 4 oz. 2 ½" Beverly cocktail glasses, and one brass plated spoon (not shown). The mixer and glasses have three platinum lines.

The 7-Piece Cocktail Hour Set #3300/178-1/12-C1, $30-40, contained one 7" shaker with plastic lid and six 3 ½ oz. 3" cocktail glasses with cherry decorations, $5-10 for the box only.

# CHAPTER THIRTEEN

# Miscellaneous Glasses

Unique Baltic glassware with etched dots and flashed red decorations. Left to right: 10 oz. footed goblet #3316, 4 5/8", $3-5; 7 oz. footed sherbet, 2 3/8", $3-5; sherbet plate, 6 1/8", $3-5.

Baltic 10 oz. #3316 goblets. Left to right: Gold Band and Hairline decoration, $3-5; unidentified decoration, $3-5; Glenmore decoration, $3-5.

Three variations of the 12 oz. handled party glasses (1955), $5-8 for each design.

Wild Geese decoration 12 oz. 5" heavy based glass (1955), $5-8.

Anchor Hocking made a myriad of these 10 oz. 4 ¾" straight shells with advertising decorations, $5-10 depending upon the specific decoration.

Rare 10 oz. 4 ¾" straight shell with a commemoration of the attack on Pearl Harbor, $30-40. There are three different views so you can see the decorations that wrap completely around the glass.

Anchor Hocking applied hundreds of decorations to glasses over the years. Here are just a few to show the variety of the decorations, $2-5 for each glass.

Set of six Gold Band and Hairline decoration shot glasses in a chrome plated holder, $35-50 for the entire set, $4-5 for each shot glass. All the shot glasses are marked with the "anchor over H" emblem.

Gay Fad decoration applied to a straight shell glass, pilsner, and #3555 goblet, $3-5 for each glass.

Yellow Rose decoration 32 oz. #3375/5703 giant iced tea, 6 7/8", $15-20.

Jelly jars with colored stars, $3-5 for each jar. The jars are marked with the "anchor over H" emblem.

Close-up of Clarion Jelly label.

Clarion Jelly was sold in at least two sizes of jars. Left to right: 14 oz. jar, 6 ¼", $3-5; 16 oz. jar, 6 ½", $3-5.

Just a few of the decorations applied on Clarion Jelly jars, $3-5 for each jar.

Just a few of the decorations applied on Clarion Jelly jars, $3-5 for each jar.

Two more Clarion Jelly jars, $3-5. I have no idea how many decorations were made. All the jars are marked with the "anchor over H" emblem.

Through the years I have accumulated a variety of pitchers and glasses I have been unable to definitively identify. Many of these have the "feel" and color of Anchor Hocking's glass. I will offer one free autographed copy of this book to the first person that can identify any of the items shown below. To qualify, I will need a company catalog reference, advertising sheet, or other documentation that, in my opinion, establishes what the item is and who made it. Gook luck!

This pitcher can be found in green, yellow, and crystal. It was probably made in the 1950s.

This pitcher can be found in crystal and yellow. It was probably made in the 1940s.

I have not been able to identify the pitcher on the left. Hazel Atlas made the pitcher on the right.